A Life of Miracles

Conference addresses on difficult subjects

Edgar (Ted) Stubbersfield

CONTENTS

INTRODUCTION

Back in 1994 I wrote a small book entitled "Pain and a Powerful God". My wife had been ill for some time and I wrote on suffering in an attempt to "put to sleep a few demons". I then photocopied a few copies and gave them to friends. My pastor told me that it was too complicated for most pastors in my denomination (in Australia) to understand.

A little while later I heard from Noe Galzote, a friend of one of the friends I had given a copy to. Noe was a Bible school principal in Manila but was running a conference in General Santos City in Southern Mindanao. He loved my book and wanted me to come to the conference to give the message. I gladly accepted. When there I met for the first time another speaker Fred Kornis, now of Heartland International Ministries. He and Noe have become close friends.

Nothing could have prepared me for that conference. The gathering was not of seminary trained men but of tribal pastors, few if any had any theological training. They just went where the trained men would not go, accepting poverty, lack of health care and education for their children for the sake of Christ. I realized I was in the presence of better men than myself. Far from being too complicated, these men hung on every word. A former guerilla fighter gave me a note saying "Brother you have blessed us".

I was introduced to real poverty. Noe told me how on a break from the college he came back home to Southern Mindanao and went to a service in one of the tribal churches. The church was no more than four posts and a thatched roof. The pastor, in bare feet, was preaching passionately from his old tattered paperback bible. A strong wind came up and blew his pages away. He had to stop mid sermon and run after his pages. That day, Noe resolved to do what he could to help these men and women who serve faithfully with so little.

At the end of the conference Noe gave each delegate a hard bound Bible, for many their first and some study tools and a copy of my book.

Fred and I were asked if we could financially assist the former guerilla. It was explained that he had opportunity to have Bible studies with his former comrades but that they had to do it at night. He needed a pressure lamp. It was only a very modest sum but it represented nine months offerings to his church. I learnt how very small sums can make big differences to someone's ministry.

I have since spoken at two other conferences organized by Noe. I was given the difficult subjects and I put a lot of work into them so I am presenting them for you with the hope that they might be of use to you as you face some of this world's difficult challenges.

Reader, I would urge you to discover the joy and deep friendships that result when you partner with a national pastor. If you want a name, contact Fred Kornis at Heartland International Ministries and he will assist. His phone number is +1 913 5152370.

1 USEFUL TIPS FOR SPEAKING OVERSEAS

When I speak in Australia, it is as a layman to a mostly white Anglo-Saxon congregation that know me well. They understand Australian humor and don't notice the accent. So, as long as I keep the sermon under 20 minutes, everything goes well. But speaking overseas in a third world is a challenge as you are outside of your comfort zone.

The following considerations prompt my preparation and delivery. They might prove useful to someone speaking overseas. They work for me.

1. Remember that you are talking to people who are probably far more faithful than yourself. Many will have followed Christ at great personal cost. Even attending the meetings may have been a sacrifice through traveling long distances, perhaps even on foot. They deserve your very best. Prepare as you have never prepared in your life before.

2. Remember that many will probably be able to read English well enough but will take in little of what you say as your English will sound very little like the English they learn in school.

3. Remember your poor translator as he will have the same trouble with your accent. Make life easy for him.

4. Remember, they will not understand your humor.

5. Remember, you will never see these people again. Don't "waffle on" and keep repeating yourself. Say it once only and move on. You will never have a chance to say what you have left out through repetition.

How I deal with this is to prepare my talk word for word. It ruins spontaneity but the tradeoff is substance. I then prepare two copies of this talk, one single line and the other double spaced and in uppercase. I send the talk off in advance and pay to have copies made for everybody attending.

The uppercase version is what I use to deliver my address. Uppercase and large print is needed as lighting might be poor. The page numbers will be different to the handouts so I mark on my copy where the page breaks are in the handouts. My word for word copy makes it very easy for the translator as he does not have to remember. You can speak in paragraphs rather than sentences. Indicate on the page with your finger how far you will speak so he knows when to start translating.

As I give the address I make it very clear when we leave one of their pages and start another so they can follow closely and not get lost. Normally you want eye contact but if the eye contact is on notes which they are concentrating on, that is excellent. You are communicating far better.

When the delegates leave they take with them a document you have poured your heart and soul into. They can then share this with their congregations so your labour is magnified. In 2009 up in the hills of Southern Mindanao I met a young pastor named Zaldi. He was my very young bodyguard when I first went to General Santos City, the bombing capital of the Philippines. He told me how, when he went back to his church, he preached from the book we gave out, *Pain and a Powerful God*. Zaldi said of his congregation, "How they wept when they acknowledged the reality of their suffering." Then he went on to say, "Oh how they wept when they acknowledged the greatness of God's grace in their suffering." He thanked me for giving him this book. This is what makes conference speaking so worthwhile.

High quality notes are the best thing that you can leave your hearers.

2 A MIRACULOUS LIFE FOR THE BELIEVER

Background to this message

In 2005 I was asked to address two topics at Christian Life Centres International (Philippines) national conference at Bokawan, Baguio City. The conference was organised by my friend Noe Galzote. Being a layman I was given the "easy" subjects, "A Miraculous Life for the Believer" and "Suffering and an Omnipotent God"

I was very grateful for the help of my friend Pastor Geoff Kuchel then of Peace Lutheran Church, Gatton, for help with these difficult subjects. This message was given as a sermon which lasted an hour. It was well received by the Philippine pastors and laymen who attended but not by the visiting Australian pastors. You can be the judge.

Acts 17;26 He made from one the whole human race to dwell on the entire surface of the earth, and he fixed the ordered seasons and the boundaries of their regions, 27 so that people might seek God, even perhaps grope for him and find him, though indeed he is not far from any one of us. 28 For 'In him we live and move and have our being,' as even some of your poets have said, 'For we too are his offspring.

Introduction –Are there miracles?

A miraculous life for the believer - There is no more difficult subject than the subject of the spectacular miracles and it needs a man far wiser and more spiritual than me to preach on it. But if what I was told back in the 70's when I was converted was right, it could be a very easy subject. I could finish it in 5 minutes. I was told that the age of miracles had passed. The people that told me this were not unbelieving liberals but very well meaning and sincere Christians. They even quoted a scripture to prove this, 1 Cr 13:8-12. They said that gifts of miracles like all the gifts of the Spirit all passed away when the scriptures were completed. There were no miracles in their own Christian life and this justified their theology. Miracles didn't happen and it was even wrong to ask for them. The God of the New Testament period who was then actively involved in the lives of his saints has now become a God who is unavailable. A God who is always unavailable for all intents and purposes might as well not exist. We now see in certain areas of the church that belief in God let alone belief in miracles is optional. The justification that miracles don't happen now is now because they never happened at all.

A miraculous life for the believer – this is what we want Brother Ted - to live and move and have our being in God as our text says must mean to live in move in the miraculous. You may say that you want a miraculous life but I can assure you that you don't. I hope that none of you ever see a miracle, at least the type of miracle you are thinking about. I hope that Christian Life Churches or the church that you represent is a group that never sees the miraculous. I hope that none of you ever has to ask for a miracle – because there is nothing that sees a miracle but misery and may misery never come knocking on your door. Sadly I know misery will be an unwelcome visitor to many here and the faith of many here will be challenged. For some your faith will be strengthened but also for some it will be bruised. For many of you, the only thing that will satisfy the deep cry of your soul is a miracle. Fortunately miracles are not that unusual. The 1996 National church Life Surveys in Australia showed that among Protestants:

	% Most significant experience	% who have such experience often	% who have this experience often or occasionally
Answer to prayer in Unusual circumstances	17	28	79
Through a specific call to action	3	16	63
By deliverance from evil	3	17	61
Deep conviction of guilt over sin	3	22	68
Vivid mystical experience	4	4	27
Miraculous healing	3	4	25
Flow of daily life	44		
No experience	11		

I expect the percentage is higher in the Philippines.

I have a very good friend Eric. He was the pastor of the Lutheran church in my home town. He became a soul mate, a friend that I could can share my inner thoughts with. I will mention him a couple of times in this sermon. I hope you all find a friend like this. I had learnt a lot in my years in Bible College and from doing correspondence. Eric stood outside that tradition and made me think again about what I was taught, and what I thought and believed. It was like someone adjusting the focus of a telescope bringing it all together in a clearer picture. Brother Noe can say the same about his time in the Presbyterian seminary. I had always thought of the miraculous as the ultimate in the Christian experience.

It was my friend that taught me how small these events are that you would call the miraculous, I will call them the spectacular miracles. I came to see also that where we should see the really miraculous is in the ordinary day to day Christian life. One day Eric said to me ,"Ted, we Lutherans are more Pentecostal that you Pentecostals". This was a shock, but he then explained what he meant. "When one of our members is sick we ask God to heal them and he does. We don't make a song and dance about it we just get on with what God has called us to do – to be his light and salt in our community". The miracle was not an end in itself but simply a tool, and a somewhat unremarkable one. Australians are always having by-passes – heart bypasses and they categorize them – double, triple, quadruple bypasses. They had one member I heard called triple by-pass Fred – not because of heart surgery but three times the church's prayer had drawn him back from the gates of heaven. The church had more work to do and Fred was needed.

At about 400 AD the great Saint Augustine, Bishop of Hippo in North Africa wrote about miracles in a book called *The City of God*. This was 300 years after I was told that miracles had disappeared. Augustine tells how each church under his control had to record the miracles that occurred in their midst and read them out to the congregation. One church recorded over 70 miracles in a two year period. We read a number of those miracles in that book. One I love - A member of his congregation was healed of breast cancer and went to see her physician. Augustine wrote: "When he had heard her account of what had happened, his voice and expression suggested, we are told that he thought little of it, so much so that she was afraid that he might make some insulting remark about Christ. But he replied …: "Why, I thought you were going to tell me something remarkable!" And when she looked horrified at this he hastily added, what is so remarkable in Christ's healing a cancer, when he once raised to life a man four days dead?" Augustine also wrote "For he that made from five loaves, bread to fill so many thousands was the same who daily prepares mighty harvests in the earth from but a few grains. For this too is a miracle of God, although we have ceased to wonder at it because it comes about day by day". Augustine just like my friend was concerned that we no longer see where the outstanding miracles lie.

"Ordinary" miracles

Let me tell you about what many of you have ceased to wonder at, these ordinary miracles. "You have been prayed for by name in the Assembly of God's people and your petition has been brought before the throne of Almighty God." You and I would say "We prayed for you in Church today" But my friend Eric, the Lutheran pastor said things very differently, I had asked him to visit my father in law, Bob in hospital. The doctors had told us that his death was near and, as Bob had no interest in things of the Lord, we were concerned. So my friend came and he said "You have been prayed for by name in the Assembly of God's people and your petition has been brought before the throne of Almighty God." The end result – our Christian doctor said "I hesitate to use the word miraculous but it is not far from it."

Bob was prayed back from the gates of death but that is not the true miracle in this story. Old Bob had been ministered to many times by godly men and it appeared to have no impact, but that day Eric's words cut right to his old dying heart Bob replied "Why would you do that for me, I am an old man. I have had my life I am not worth anything". "What are you saying old man, Don't you know your very precious to God? His son died for you and he wants you to stand in his presence". Eric kept visiting over the next 9 months and one day he asked Bob if he was now trusting Jesus, "Yes", "Would you like communion"? "Yes" and 2 days before he died we had communion as a family in an atmosphere that was charged with God's salvation. There is the miracle – an old man, not worth anything was so loved by his God that he made certain that Bob would stand in his presence forever.

If you want to see a miracle – look around you at the assembly of God's people. Each and every one of you is the special object of God's love. Some of us, myself included, who have grown up in the church have been forgiven little. What I mean is: you do not come from a life of violence, drunkenness, immorality and you looked almost as good unsaved as you do saved. Because of that we run the risk of not seeing what a miracle we are and of loving our savior little. While people never say it aloud I have seen an attitude in the church which says "I chose for Christ, by my strength I have lived a good life and I will have earned a great reward when I stand before him". Those of you who have been forgiven much know what I am saying, of how amazing and how miraculous God's grace is. Our Father set his love upon us when we were his enemies.

The scripture is very clear, we, even the very best of us, were once his enemies. Our father was once the Devil and yet God and God alone has taken us from the kingdom of darkness to the kingdom of light and made us his friends. This work of grace in your life is all his doing. The only thing that you offer to this partnership is the sin that the blood of Christ saves you from. The Father gives you everything. A miraculous life for the believer starts in accepting God's forgiveness and the miraculous life continues by claiming God's forgiveness daily. It takes a miracle of faith to stop working at being good enough. It take a miracle to accept a life which is all of grace. Until you really have this miracle in your heart any miracle in your body means little just as it did for Bob. Think of the healing of the 10 lepers – only one, the one with the least right to a miracle, the Samaritan, came back and thanked Jesus. The miracle did the nine no lasting good.

Have you ever considered what a miracle prayer is? Not answered prayer, but just prayer itself. Do you pray? Of course you do but probably most people in this world do also. But what do they pray to? I was visiting a national park once and there at the base of a really magnificent tree was a group of women burning candles and chanting. The ranger I was with asked them what are you doing - "We are honoring this tree." Honoring a tree? These weren't ignorant savages but educated people in a so called civilized society. I have seen people pray to trees and rocks and idols of stone. I have seen people pray to other gods Allah, or Buddha. What names and things have people prayed to in your country over its long history? They have all thought that by their many words that God must hear them and when he doesn't some even cut their body or otherwise punish themselves.

Some people go to their priests to hear from their god for them. We and we alone pray to the living God. There is no priest, just the God who created this universe and you and I the very least of his creation. We do not stand outside the gates of heaven saying "Saint Peter, could you take this message into Mary and have her ask Jesus to give it to the father for me". None of us could come anywhere near the president of this country and tell her your problems. Yet we are told to come boldly into God's presence and stand before him and make our requests directly to him, face to face with the creator of this universe. What's more there is no time limit. You will say that answered prayer is miracle and it is but I expect the greater miracle is the fact that we can we can pray to the living God and that God not only tolerates us but wants us to come before him.

To the pastors among you - how do you consider the ministry of the word and sacraments? Historically as Pentecostals we have been strong as preachers of the word and weak on sacraments. Now, in Australia, many ministers are weak in both the word and sacraments. I have heard sermons taken from the internet and communion treated as nothing more than an unwelcome intrusion into an hour of song singing. My friend Eric once challenged me about this as well – he said that the only things that God has given him as a minister of the Gospel that is different to his congregation is the ministry of the word and sacraments and to fulfill his ministry he had to be strong in both word and sacrament.

He was right. We have an expression "as busy as a one armed wall paper hanger". There are some things that take two hands. The ministry of the gospel needs power in both word and sacrament. Any one in your churches can pray, anyone can visit the sick, anyone can do good works. Not only can they do these things but it should be the duty of everyone to do them, and better still if they do them out of their nature. But not everyone is called to minister the word and the sacraments.

God could have chosen any way he wanted to grow his church but he has chosen the foolishness of preaching. In Australia I have seen movements come and go but God's word remains the same. He has chosen the foolishness of preaching, the gospel spoken and the gospel acted in the sacraments. When you leave the pulpit do you say, "I hope I have preached Gods word" or "I have preached God's word". When you preach do you just tickle the ears of your members or is a deep work done in the lives of men and women.

Are sins forgiven, are attitudes changed, do men and women find the strength to live holy lives, does your congregation find strength in times of trouble, and are people reconciled? Do men and women find the strength to die well?

Do you think that this your eloquence? Some people are eloquent. It is said of George Whitfield, one of the leading preachers of the Great Awakening in the 1700's in England and North America that he could bring a man to tears by the way he said "Mesopotamia" but tears don't save. My favorite hymn *Rock of Ages* says

Could my tears for ever flow
All for sin could not atone
Thou must save and thou alone.

Your abilities have done none of this, it is God that saves and it is God that changes. It is all a miracle that he lets you be part of. My friends, if you don't have this miracle when you preach don't look for signs of wonders. Give God no peace until you posses this gift above all gifts. A sinner reconciled is of more value than a body healed.

Does Christ come in a special way when you gather in his name? Does the creator of this universe stand in your midst? Is he here now? We know that sometimes his presence is so real it is as if you can reach out and touch him. Of course I am always the odd man out. Often our pastor will say "There is a wonderful presence of God in this place" and everybody will say "Amen". All except me, I feel nothing. Yet I know he is there because he has promised to be here.

That Christ will come even closer when he speaks to us through his word and when he offers us his broken body and spilt blood this is miraculous. It is a miracle when his life becomes our life.

I have seen how powerful it is to declare a man's sins forgiven and also to tell him that his sins are not forgiven. We who were once Christ's enemies can now stand in his place and say "If you are trusting in Jesus your sins are forgiven" or to say the opposite "If you are not trusting in Jesus your sins are not forgiven". Have you seen the change in the life of a man whose sins are forgiven? Don't you consider it a miracle that the greatest of sinners can be given the assurance that he is a new person and that the old has passed away. It is a miracle that he can have locked in his heart the unshakable assurance that those things that separated him from his Father will never accuse him again?

One of the ways we live a miraculous life is in the way God leads us, with the friends we make, our life partner, and work. There is no end to the areas God leads us in. Proverbs 3:5-6 says "Trust in the Lord with all your heart and lean not on your own understanding: In all your ways acknowledge him and he will make your paths straight". In my past I have struggled over some decisions, and not known what to do. To know the right thing to do was beyond me and yet when I look back it was clear that God was directing me. When we place our hands in his and ask him to lead us we enter into a life of the miraculous.

If I have a favorite doctrine it is the doctrine of Providence. I had never heard about it in the circles I moved in till I was 23 years old and I went to a little Baptist chapel in country England. They named their chapel "Providence". By the time I left them 2 years later I had come to respect God's providence and, as I got older, I came to love it. One definition is "Providence is the universal sovereign reign of God. It is God's preserving and governing all his creatures, and all their actions (Job 9:5,6; 28:25; Ps. 104:10-25; 145:15; 147:9; Matt. 4:4; 6:26-28; Luke 12:6,7; Acts 17:25-28).

Providence is in two parts **General providence** includes the government of the entire Universe, especially the affairs of men. **Special providence** is God's particular care over the life and activity of the Believer (Rom. 8:28)". You do not live in a world that is chaotic even though it looks that way, and your life is not governed by chance or fate.

This world is working to a purpose and an end which includes your best interests. The miracle of **General providence** is that God has not allowed the world to continue unrestrained in its self-destruction. The miracle of **Special providence** is that I have not destroyed myself. God has reached into my world and prevented the natural consequence of my sin from destroying me. The more I trust in God's care for me, the more I am certain that he is ordering the events of my life for my good. The more I trust him the more I see his hand of care over me.

Providence, pastors do you preach and teach providence? Don't be afraid of doing a doctrinal sermon on the subject. I vividly recall the first time I did. I was not aware that three of our church members had to sell their home over the next week to avoid severe difficulties. I was told afterwards by the pastor, who initially thought it was a strange choice of subject, that they all sold. Providence is nothing less than a miracle and you live in it every minute of every day. Every day of your life and mine is a witness to God's loving and miraculous care of us.

In the Lord's Prayer, Jesus taught us to say "Lead us not into temptation but deliver us from evil." Have you ever been kept from sin? There is an enemy of your soul, have no doubt about that, and that enemy wants nothing better than to destroy you just as he wanted to destroy Peter on the night of the last supper. I have seen men that I thought were giants in the faith crash through sin, generally through immorality but the most dangerous I have seen is pride. I have also seen men restore their lives and their faith after a moral lapse but I have not seen a man recover from fall caused by pride.

I expect that I am not as spiritual as the other speakers because I have to fight my flesh daily. I know what it is to reach the end of my strength and to take my eyes from the source of that strength. But we don't just struggle in own strength and when my will and my strength had left me, deliverance came from a source I could have never imagined. Why me Father and not the others? I don't know. But God's hand was over me that day and Jesus prayed for me as he prayed for Peter. Being kept from sin is a miracle as real and as precious as any miracle of healing. Do you look to our Lord to keep you from sin or are you struggling with just your own strength?

You already have a miraculous life. But you are probably saying, Brother Ted, this is all too ordinary, I wanted to hear about signs and wonders and raising the dead. Yes it is ordinary, so ordinary that we do not recognize how special and miraculous it is. It is so ordinary that even non believers have shared in this blessing. Our text says "in him we live and move and have our being". Aren't these the great words of Paul? No!! He was quoting the Greek poet Epimenides (6th c. BC), from his *Hymn to Zeus.* Our text goes on to say *"*For we are his offspring": again it is not Paul but comes from at least two Greek poets Aratus (c. 270 BC), in a poem *Phaenomena* and Kleanthes (331-233 BC) in a *Hymn to Zeus.* These words are straight out of paganism hundreds of years before Paul. How can it be?

Jesus said that God send his rain on the just and the unjust. If the heathen as they groped for God trying to find him could recognize that there was something special about the ordinary life then how much more should we. We have the clear revelation of the Father through the Son and we have the Spirit to teach us. We should be able to see far better the mighty, miraculous hand of our loving

Father at work in our life? In him we live and move in the miraculous because we are his offspring.

Spectacular miracles in perspective

But what about the spectacular miracles? This is what we want to see. There are probably there are two groups here. Some might say we already see miracles in our meetings, we already have signs, now we want wonders. We even want to go up a level to the raising of the dead. I say to you "Stop"! Have you understood what you already possess? You are not ready to move on until you do. What of the second group, those of you who do not see many miracles in your church. Learn to trust him in the small things first, you want to run, learn to walk first. Understand that trusting God for the spectacular miracles is in no way different to way you trust God and walk in the miraculous every day. It is all of grace. To the preachers I say – give care to your craft so that God will bless it with signs and wonders following.

My friends, don't think that a miracle is going to solve your problems. Perhaps, for some who experience a miracle, your problems will just be starting. Take blind Bartemaeus. He has been begging all his life and one day Jesus comes into his life and opens his eyes. Can you imagine his joy? The man is extremely happy, the people are praising god and it is a wonderful day. He goes to bed a very happy man and in the morning he wakes up and reaches out for his beggars bowl and then it dawns on him. Who is going to give money to a perfectly able bodied man? The only thing he knows to do is to beg and this is taken from him. Now as a grown man without any skills he has to earn a living. The miracle did not solve all his problems it gave him different ones and possibly even bigger ones. But no matter what his circumstance were, he would say "God came into my life and showed me that he was bigger than my problems and that he cared for me". The problems came into perspective. It didn't solve them, it made them manageable.

I once met a woman who said she had been raised from the dead. During a serious sickness she had made quite an impression on an unbelieving surgeon but after an operation she died. She said how this unbelieving surgeon kneeled over her body and took issue with God asking him why did he let it happen to someone who trusted him as she did. The woman said that as the doctor said these words her body stirred. Other people were there that knew the woman and not one indicated to me that she was a little strange in the head. One even said it was true and perhaps it was. Let me tell you another story, one I know to be true. The daughter of a former missionary died. I think she had been a missionary too. The old man was so certain that God would raise her from the dead he took a change of clothes to the cemetery at the burial. There was no resurrection. Raising the dead, why would you do it even if you could?

My old friend Eric again put things in perspective for me. One day he had to bury a young mother, (our neighbor) and an elder from his church. The Gideons, of which I am a member, were to receive donations to purchase Bibles in memory of those two. I went to Eric before the first service to run through Gideon matters with him. I said, "Sad day Eric" and he corrected me very strongly, "No Ted, it is a glorious day" He explained himself, "These two have been faithful unto death and now stand in God's presence, my responsibility to them as a pastor has been discharged. No Ted, it is a glorious day" My own pastor asked me if my wife Rachel died wouldn't I ask God to bring her back to life? No, she is safely home. My friends, believe the gospel! Do not let the sadness of the day of mourning rob you of the certainty of how glorious the day is. Our Lord is only asking us to go where he has gone, he asks us to commit our spirit into his Father's hands just as he did. The grave with all horrors has been sanctified by Christ's presence. The ability to die well is the greatest miracle you will experience apart from your conversion.

What do you say when a child is ill and its life is at risk. Do you call the church to prayer and intercede on behalf of the child and the parents? Do you knock on the door of heaven and give God no peace just like the widow and the unjust judge. Will God give you your petition just to get some peace irrespective of the rights and wrongs of the case? We who know and understand so little and have virtually no control over things come before God who knows everything, is all powerful and above all is complete in wisdom and makes no mistakes and say, change your mind. Is this an act of great faith or great foolishness and presumption? It could be either.

Years ago when I was being taught about miracles in the UK the lecturer an old pastor told this story about when he was a young pastor. A young baby, the child of a church member was dying and nothing could be done. The church as called to prayer and the child was miraculously healed and all glorified God. Years later the mother would live to see her child hung. His life was forcibly taken for taking the life of another. That mother regretted the day she called the church to pray without seeking the Lord's will. The sorrow of losing a child into the fathers care was nothing compared to losing him as an adult under these circumstances into an uncertain destiny.

When do you pray, when do you trust the almighty hand of God? I don't know the answer. The spectacular miracles of God carry with them a tremendous burden, that of accepting the hand of God in all things! It means accepting that it is God's decision whether to heal or not to heal, whether to provide or not to provide. The true miracle of life is to see the hand of God in the daily activities of our life, to recognize the love of God in the simple things of living, the fall of the rain, caring for an old man, the repentance of a husband for his anger directed at his wife and children, the daily bread which fills our plate, We must also see the true miracle of life in the bread and wine of communion and the water of baptism which splashes life into our lives.

3 SUFFERING AND AN OMNIPOTENT GOD

Background to this message

In 2005 I was asked to address two topics at Christian Life Centres International (Philippines) National Conference at Bokawan, Baguio City. The conference was organised by my friend Noe Galzote. Being a layman I was given the "easy" subjects, "A Miraculous Life for the Believer" and "Suffering and an Omnipotent God" My friend Fred Kornis eas also one of the speakers.

I was very grateful for the help of my friend Pastor Geoff Kuchel then of Peace Lutheran Church, Gatton, for help with these difficult subjects. This message was given in a lecture format which lasted an hour.

Luke 13:1-5   Now there were some present at that time who told Jesus about the Galileans whose blood Pilate had mingled with their sacrifices.   2. Jesus answered "do you think that these Galileans were worse sinners than all the other Galileans because they suffered this way?"   3. I tell you, No! But unless you repent, you too will all perish.   4. Or those eighteen who died when the tower in Siloam fell on them – Do you think they were more guilty than all the others living in Jerusalem? 5. I tell you, no! But unless you repent you too will all perish.

Omnipotence and suffering – Thank you brother Noe for giving me the easy subjects. I am only a poor business man, a layman, which is why I was given the simple talk.

1. At first glance suffering seems simple

Our text covers the range of human pain. Man made with the slaughter of the Galileans by Pilate and natural with a collapsing tower. This text also confronts us with the disciples desire to have a nice and simple theology of suffering – cause and effect. Do you think they were worse sinners? Of course they did. The disciples had a theology that did not tax their faith. In fact they wanted a faith that did not require any faith. We see the same in John 9:1 Rabbi, who sinned this man or his parents that he was born blind? If you sin you suffer, if you are suffering you have sinned. God is just like us, made in our image and easy to understand. Just like he was easy to understand with the boxing day Tsunami when 250,000 were killed.

During the first days the images of the wave were overwhelming. There were thousands of Australians unaccounted for. My nation was deeply moved. The government gave $1B to Indonesia and the Australian people gave hundreds of millions. The charity I support, Doctors without Borders told me when I rang, "We do not need any more money."

Quickly the media were asking leading ministers, was this the judgment of God? People wanted answers. Look who were killed. There were over 200,000 Muslims killed in Indonesia. *Christianity Today* quotes *Operation World* saying that there were only 50 Aceh Christians and most in provinces outside the affected area. In Sri Lanka there were 30,000 deasths, predominantly Buddhists and Hindu's. In India the Hindus were affected. The Christian countries were left untouched.

This is so easy to see, some would have said, God's judgment on his enemies. This is simple cause and effect. Many would be grateful to see a reason as they believe God is just and understandable. Scripture is very clear, there can be a direct link of cause and effect, between sin and punishment.   In this case it is so easy to allow ourselves see a connection.

2. The paradox of suffering

It is easy to see a connection **providing we don't look to closely**. Were the Moslems of Ache worse than most Moslems?   Certainly they were militant.   Were they worse sinners than the Muslims of Mindanao.   There were many Christians in the fishing villages of Batak Aceh as they had a strong Lutheran community – Not the 50 total for the whole of Aceh.   It has been suggested that on a percentage basis Christians took a heavier toll than the Moslems. Abraham said to the Lord in Gen 18:23 Will you sweep away the righteous with the wicked?   What if there are 50 righteous in the city? Will you really sweep it away and not spare the place for the sake of 50 righteous people in it?   Far be it from you to do such a thing – to kill the righteous with the wicked, treating the righteous and the wicked alike.   Far be it from you!   Will not the judge of the earth do right?   Yet a Lutheran pastor in Aceh can only stand in remains of his empty church and say "You have treated the righteous and wicked alike – why"?

If you can't understand that, try the 1755 Lisbon earthquake.   It shook the church to its core.   It took place on November 1, 1755. This quake was estimated at 9 on Richter scale, the same as Indonesia.   Note the date November 1, that is All Saints Day.   We Pentecostals don't keep saints days and don't see the importance of the day. All Saints Day is a universal Christian Feast that honours and remembers all Christian saints, known and unknown   The Lisbon earthquake happened at 9:20 when thousands of people were in stone churches. This wasn't just a natural disaster as there could not have been a more significant time or place.   On the eve of All Saints Day in 1517 Luther nailed his 95 thesis on the castle church door of Wittenburg and started the reformation almost 500 years ago. He chose that day as he wanted to say I am not starting something new, I stand with what has gone before me, that the church, despite its problems, is good and holy. Was this now God's judgment on Christianity? Was God saying everything that has gone before was bad and not worth remembering and honoring. It is said that the catholic priests roamed streets looking for suspected heretics and hung them on sight. There must be a reason for the pain, surely God was judging Catholic Church for allowing heretics to live. When we look back do we say, "Was God judging the Catholic Church", and it did need radical change. But it is harder to make excuses for God because there would have been many, many good and godly people in church that day. Those that were not crushed under their collapsing churches were burnt and those who escaped the flames were drowned in the tidal wave just as in Indonesia. 100,000 perished that day.

What then do we say of the genocide of the Armenians which occurred between 1915 to 1919 when Moslem Turks murdered somewhere around 1.5m Armenians. Their only crime was being Christians. The Armenians were the first country to accept Christ. To be an Armenian was to be a Christian. A contemporary writer said "In vain do we strain our ears to hear some voice from the throne of the Divine Majesty. The far off heaven where, in perfect peace and unutterable glory, God dwells and reigns, is SILENT."

3. Is suffering relevant to you?

Is this talk about a God who just does he wishes – and that is a very good definition of omnipotence the fact that God can do as he wishes - just an interesting tickling of your intellect. I don't think so. I believe it is vital to you in understanding your own suffering and the suffering of your nation. I did not have to look far to realise the words *disaster* and *Philippines* almost go hand in hand. According to the Philippine Red Cross, 31,835 Filipinos were killed and 94,369,462 others were affected by natural disasters and calamities in a span of 20 years The Philippine National Red Cross governor Dante Liban said. "The Philippines was a natural laboratory for floods, typhoons, monsoon rains, earthquakes, volcanic eruptions, and landslides,". (Source: Philippine Daily Inquirer)

Data from the Disaster Response Operations Monitoring and Information Center (DROMIC) showed that there were 313 disaster incidents in the country in 2002, up from only 199 incidents in 2001. In particular, there were 120 fire incidents that affected 15,430 households in 2002, 63 deportation or relocation incidents, 22 armed conflicts that distressed 8,891 families, 22 bombing incidents or explosions, 22 flashfloods that affected 234,414 households, and 7 destructive typhoons that distressed 568,345 families. Other types of disasters that happened in 2002 were vehicular accidents, sea mishap, tornado, massacre, plane crash, and earthquakes.

Your nation has suffered. Has suffering come near to you? Have you suffered personally, or your loved ones. Is the suffering any easier if the losses are smaller? The hand of the omnipotent God will come near to many of you if it has not done so already. What will you say, what will you do? Will you sit like Job and complain that God is unjust because the righteous suffer along with the wicked. Will you say "what is point of being righteous."

What did the prophets of old say when they saw disaster looming - it was repentance. When these troubles eventually overwhelmed their nation – was their message retribution? – No it was a call to repentance. Only through repentance – and repentance is simply a call to draw near to god - could they have hope in the midst of despair and life in the midst of death. Has the message changed?

Brother Fred (Kornis) as an American has had to confront our text in the falling Twin Towers of New York. After 9/11 we heard two messages – one was a call for retribution. This is the same call that would have come from the Galileans after some of their countrymen were killed by Pilate offering sacrifices. The other call was for national repentance. If Jesus was teaching in New York he might well have said, "Do you think that those who died in the towers were worse sinners than all the others in New York?" If Jesus were here now he might well say "Were the 500 who died when they were buried alive when a tower of garbage collapsed at the Payatas dumpsite in Quezon City worse sinners than all those who lived in Quezon City"? Do you want a simple answer to pain and suffering – they got what they deserve - then Jesus says OK you can keep it, now repent for you are no better.

4. Excuses we make for God

People have always been trying to make excuses for God. Some would say that there is the good God of Jesus Christ who is responsible for everything good. For the bad things there is some other force, named or unnamed, perhaps it is the devil or his demons but God will have none of that. The buck stops at the throne of heaven and God accepts that

Isa 45:7 I form the light and I create darkness, I bring prosperity and create disaster, I the Lord do these things.

Some would say that the problem lies in mans free will, God did not do these things but man who has the power to choose good and evil, wisdom or foolishness, life or death. Reform man and the choices he makes and the problems will be solved. There will be no more war, no more poverty no more injustice. But God said that the heart of man does not need a doctor and a therapy but it needs a savior for it is hopelessly bound outside of the quickening by the Holy Spirit.

I have heard people say about suffering that we cannot understand because God's ways are different to ours. But isn't that really saying that God is unknowable? If so, we may as well give up trying to know God now. But surely the difference between a believer and God a difference in degree and not in nature? If you have seen a young child draw a circle it isn't much like a circle but the connection is there, it is still a circle that was attempted. Our father has revealed himself to us as a holy God and from that we understand our own need for holiness. We can strive for holiness and we will fall short of it but our failure will be one of degree not nature.

The Roman Cicero's apology for Jupiter's neglect of the world was that "the sovereign of the universe is on the whole a good sovereign, but with so much business on his hands that he has not time to look into details". But Lord will not have that said of him. Look at the scriptures:

Luke 12:7 *The hairs of your head are numbered*
Matt 10:29 *Are not two sparrows sold for a penny Yet not one of them will fall to the ground apart from the will of your father*
Luke 12:6 *Are not five sparrows sold for two pennies. Even the sparrow that is thrown in for free because it has such little value will not fall without our fathers will.*
Matt 6 25:34 [25] *"Therefore I tell you, do not worry about your life, what you will eat or drink; or about your body, what you will wear. Is not life more than food, and the body more than clothes?* [26] *Look at the birds of the air; they do not sow or reap or store away in barns, and yet your heavenly Father feeds them. Are you not much more valuable than they?* [27] *Can any one of you by worrying add a single hour to your life?*

[28] "And why do you worry about clothes? See how the flowers of the field grow. They do not labor or spin. [29] Yet I tell you that not even Solomon in all his splendor was dressed like one of these. [30] If that is how God clothes the grass of the field, which is here today and tomorrow is thrown into the fire, will he not much more clothe you—you of little faith? [31] So do not worry, saying, 'What shall we eat?' or 'What shall we drink?' or 'What shall we wear?' [32] For the pagans run after all these things, and your heavenly Father knows that you need them. [33] But seek first his kingdom and his righteousness, and all these things will be given to you as well. [34] Therefore do not worry about tomorrow, for tomorrow will worry about itself. Each day has enough trouble of its own.

These verses clearly show a God who says he takes care of the details! The Lord says he is not too busy to look into the details of your life and mine. But make no mistake, there were many Christians killed in the Indian Ocean Tsunami. On boxing day many were in church when the wave hit. One church in eastern Sri Lanka lost all but three worshipers and another all but one. A pastor said "I keep hearing of more and more wonderful Christians who have died" (Christianity Today Feb 2005) In the same way there were many devout and godly Catholics in Lisbon in 1755 and also among the Armenians. In the midst of this horror God has said I have taken care of the details. We look for a kind and loving god yet often are confronted with a God that seems to delight in the torment of poor wretches and to be a fitter object for hate than for love – to quote an old Christian writer. When we ask why, why did his happen we cannot clearly distinguish been God and the devil and God becomes hidden in our speculation.

There comes a time when you run out of excuses to justify God's action. You cannot find a clear connection between cause and effect. Who sinned? Jesus said neither. There comes a time when you simply have to say "Lord I do not understand. Why don't You make these things clear in your word", yet he leaves us one word – "Repent", the call to draw near to him.

5. WHEN GOD HIDES FROM US

We know that God is invisible and that we cannot see Him. Despite being invisible we can be very conscious of Him, the universe displays his glory for us to see easily. There comes a time like the tsunami however when God really is invisible and his creation shows none of his grace and glory. Could God deliberately hide himself from us? That is just what Isaiah says in the continuation of the passage we read earlier in verse 15, Truly you are a God who hides Himself.

How do you get you mind around such things - and our mind demands a reasonable answer. At the time of Lisbon many things were written, some even attacking the existence of God. There you are, this catastrophe when the churches are full is proof he did not exist But there were also defences of God's actions written. Liebniz a Christian and one of the greatest mathematicians of his age wrote a book called *Theodicy*. That word is used today for a defence of God in the face of suffering.

Liebniz understood the idea of infinity and argued in an infinity of possible worlds, the one we live in the best possible one. Wouldn't a world without earthquakes be better than world with one? It is only possible if the laws of physics are stood aside and that would be absolute chaos. If this is the best possible world I would hate to see the others. He argued that the extent of the disaster was only because the residents of Lisbon had disobeyed God by living in a city, not the rural surroundings we see in the OT. What are you talking about Leibnitz? Is that the best explanation you with all your intellect and powers of reason can give. Tell me Mr.

Leibnitz if this is right why were the residents of Lisbon so bad that they had to be punished and the residents of London Paris or Madrid did not.

Arguments of reason come crashing down because this was never a matter of reason and philosophy. If God cannot be found in reason it is because he never wanted to be found here by minds that are captive to sin. Rather it is a matter of faith and the Christ that has been revealed and preached. It is not something you can understand with your mind but discerned through a heart redeemed from sin. Jesus said, "Do you think they were more guilty than all the others in Jerusalem I tell you, No? But unless you repent you will all perish". Unbelief makes a judge and enemy out of God the father … faith makes a God and father out of an enemy and judge.

6. When God shows himself to us

The first time I met Fred Kornis I said something which caused him to ask me "What is the gospel". You know I had to think. I knew a lot of doctrines, I knew the father and his Son and had been helped by the Spirit on many occasions but I had to think. The Bible does not give a precise definition. There are a few text such as *The gospel is the power of god unto salvation* but what is salvation? *For God so loved the world that he gave his only begotten son etc* but what constitutes eternal life. The college I studied at spoke of the 4 square gospel where Jesus was Saviour, Healer, Baptiser in the Holy Spirit and Coming king. I gave a long answer that satisfied Fred but not me. I wanted a definition of the Gospel in less than ten words. I am a member of the Gideons and we have a saying "Keep the main thing the main thing" A good definition would help me keep the main thing the main thing. I read Luther's definition one day. He said the Gospel was The gracious promise of forgiveness in Christ Jesus. This is the gospel in just eight words.

This is what the Word of the Lord is to those who have owned him in Baptism

Matt 28:20, *I will be with you always , to the very end of the age*
Mk 16:16, *Whoever believes and is baptised will be saved (no condemnation)*
Mk:16:17-18, *Powerful abiding presence of the Holy Spirit"*
Acts 2:28, *The forgiveness of your sins*
Acts 2:29, *The salvation of your family*

There is only one thing promised to you. It is not a long and comfortable life, It is not a life without difficulties, without pain, it is not a prosperous life, It is not a life with a happy marriage and wonderful children. Just as God sends his rain on the just and the unjust the troubles of this world come without discrimination to the just and the unjust. What is promised is that if you are trusting in Christ your sins are forgiven and that as sons of God the Father Son and Holy Spirit will never forsake you.

In the uncertainty of life Christ offers you the certainty of forgiveness of your sins. Against the empty answers of the wisest philosopher the Father says "Behold this is my Son, listen to Him, look at Him as he lies in the manger and on the lap of his mother, as he hangs on the cross. Observe what he does and what he says. There you will surely take hold of Me." . Truly you are a God who hides himself but the passage goes on to say "O God and Saviour of Israel". He will not be found by you in any other place because he has chosen not to be found other than in his revelation of himself in scripture. God can only be found here because he will not bypass the revelation of our own nature as sinners.

7. Hope in the face of suffering

But Ted, you are saying that the answer is only internal, God will care for my soul but what about the external - my body, my family. Is my only hope in heaven and none in this world? It is your responsibility to look internally with God's help but it is God's responsibility with your help to care for the external. But what will the future hold, I need to know? Wouldn't it be good to know the future just like God so we can avoid the pain? Then I wouldn't have to trust him so much. The Old Testament scriptures were very clear about enquiring into the future. In many places it says that God's people were not to do it. They were not to go to people who consulted the dead, or people who interpreted the future from the insides of a animal or looked at the stars or dreamed dreams or the prophets of other gods. King George 6th in his Christmas message during the darkest days of World War 2 said these words "And I said to the man who stood at the gate of the year, 'Give me a light that I may tread safely into the unknown'. And he replied: "Go out into the darkness and put your hand into the hand of God. That shall be to you better than light and safer than a known way." He was saying, you do not need to know what tomorrow holds you need to trust God in whatever tomorrow holds, whether it be good or ill.

If you are washed out to sea by a tsunami it is pretty certain that you will die. But there is a world of difference between being washed into the loving arms of Jesus and being washed into an eternity separated from God. The internal aspect of knowing that your sins are forgiven and are at peace with God is the only thing you need to know and he gives that to you freely. Fortunately you do not have to be washed out to sea to experience that. If you can avoid the wave and your life is spared but your home and business is destroyed what do you say? Saving my soul is great but I have to eat, I have to feed my family. What do I do?

It is largely in your hands because your answer is in prayer. You needs were not much different from that of the first disciples that walked with Jesus. They had left their livelihoods behind, the nets, the tax collectors stand and they lived on charity. The disciples came to Jesus and asked him to teach them to pray. Of course they had prayed before but the prayers of men who have few needs or troubles will be different to that of men in great need. Jesus taught them to pray "give us today our daily bread" and you may have to live day by day pleading desperately for your very survival. You are treading a path that better men than you or I have walked. Every one that has gone before you has had to rely on prayer and your loving Father gave them grace and strength. I spoke before about times when God hides himself from us but this only so that we might find him again. I said that there are places you will not find the father such as speculation but there are places where he will be found and at times like this the best is prayer. Is the pain to much to pray well? Far from instructing us, as Jesus did to his disciples, the Spirit enters right into the intense emotions of the least of his children, praying to the Father as we only wished we could, Rom 8:26. "Likewise the Spirit also helps in our weakness. For we do not know what we should pray for as we aught, but the Spirit Himself makes intercession for us with groanings that cannot be uttered".

We have all been called to bear the *cross of Christ* Lk 14:27. This means living the humble life of a servant, needy, forsaken, mocked, and not loving the world. But we have also been called to bear the *yoke of Christ*. As the young oxen is yoked to the older experienced animal and the pair share the same burden, so we are to be yoked to Christ. You may think you have been given broader shoulders to bear the burden but it is actually it is a load lightened because it is shared.

Surely we could love him better if we had no load to carry. God will risk the danger that your love may grow cold because of his judgements because there is a much greater risk. That danger is that in preserving his saints they will lose their love for their guilty brothers and sisters who are bought under judgement, and that they finally will proudly say, "I am not as they are. The call to repent – a call to Christians and unbelievers alike will be wasted on them.

4 THINKING CRITICALLY ABOUT THE BIBLE

Background

My friend Fred Kornis and I were asked to speak at two conferences in the Philippines in December 2009. This was before the disastrous floods and landslides following Typhoon Kestana. A somber mood hung over the country and it was wisely considered that a subject befitting the mood was required. This address was largely finished so I include it here.

Biblical Criticism, what is it? For some scholars it is nothing short of just that, an intellectual exercise where criticisms are made against the Bible to discredit it as a source of reliable information or ethical guidance. This is not what we will be talking about for the next two hours. Biblical criticism has been defined as *the academic treatment of the bible as an historical document* and need not be, and should not be, the same thing as criticism of the Bible. Rather than standing over the scriptures and passing judgement over them, we believe that they should, instead, be passing judgement on us. Hebrews 4:3 says just this

For the word of God is quick, and powerful, and sharper than any two edged sword, piercing even to the dividing asunder of soul and spirit, and of the joints and marrow, and is a discerner of the thoughts and intents of the heart

As evangelical believers I expect we are uncomfortable with the expression "Biblical Criticism" because it sounds very close to "criticism of the Bible". And yet if you want to be a wise steward of the call our Lord has placed on your life to be a minister of his word, Biblical criticism is something that you should already be about and must continue to be about. It is something you must do very well. Our aim today is to examine how think critically, or to put it differently, the think rationally about the Bible.

The freedom you and I enjoy to worship and interpret the scriptures, in accordance with our conscience, was won through the courage and often the blood of the reformers. Without them we would not be here talking about Biblical criticism. At what was probably the reformation's most crucial point, Martin Luther, In April 1521, stood before the Diet of Worms, the parliament of the Holy Roman Empire held in the small town of Worms on the Rhine River. Here, with only his conscience to rely upon, he stood before "the massed authority of the whole world"[1] both ecclesiastical and civil. When it was demanded that he deny what he had written he said *"Unless I am convinced by testimony from the Holy Scriptures and* **clear proofs based on reason** *... I am bound by my conscience and the Word of God. Therefore I can and will recant nothing, because to act against ones conscience is neither safe nor salutary. So help me God"*.[2] Reports of what happened that day vary and some biographers say "I am bound by the Scriptures adduced by me" That is, he was bound by his understanding of the scriptures as determined by his reason. Either way there is the call for reason or deduction when applying the scriptures to our conscience and, as ministers of grace, applying it to the conscience of our congregations. But was he right to give such a high standing to reason and deduction when attempting to understand the scriptures?

In January 1525, a group of twelve men gathered in the home of Felix Manz near Zurich, Switzerland. They had been disheartened at the speed of the reformation and their zeal for reform drove them beyond the pace and extent of the changes that were occurring. All twelve were baptised by immersion and founded a new church. No other act showed the complete separation with Rome.[3] Most would eventually die for this act. So started the

---

[1] Friedenthal, Richard. *Luther*. (London: Weidenfeld and Nicolson, 1970) 273.
[2] Friedenthal. Luther…, 278.
[3] Estep, William R. *The Anabaptist Story*. (Grand Rapids: Eerdmans, 1975) 11.

Anabaptists and along with them, a very different way of looking at the scriptures. For them *Sola Scriptura* or the "Bible only" had a different meaning. It was just that "only scripture", free of tradition and scholarship. Estep, in his history of the Anabaptists says "At this point the Anabaptists were the most protestant and the furthest removed from Protestantism"[4]

This attitude towards the scriptures is a very longstanding characteristic of Baptists. The London Confession of the Baptist Church of 1689 follows, wherever possible, the Westminster Confession of the reformed church of 1647. These confessions would be unknown to you, but in the history of the church among the English speaking peoples they are very important. While there is much agreement, that is why they based their confession on the earlier one after all, they could not agree concerning the role of the believers interaction with the scriptures. The Calvinist Puritans had said that *"The whole counsel of God, concerning all things necessary for his own glory, man's salvation, faith, and life, is either expressly set down in Scripture, or by good and necessary consequence may be **deduced** from Scripture,"*[5], note the word "deduced, The Baptists strongly disagreed with this.

In their confession the Baptists revised this clause to read *"The whole counsel of God concerning all things necessary for his own glory, man's salvation, faith and life, is either expressly set down or necessarily contained in the Holy Scripture"*.[6] In the early days of the Baptist church there was no place in their scheme for deduction when interpreting the scriptures. Unlike the Catholic Church, and as you would expect, they would not accept tradition as a revelation standing alongside the scriptures as its equal. But the Baptist also disagreed with the reformers who said; *whatever is*

---

[4] Estep. *Anabaptist...*, 144.
[5] Westminster Confession of Faith 1647 1.6.
[6] *London Baptist Confession of 1689* 1.6.

not prohibited in scripture is permissible, saying instead *that which is not commanded is not required.*[7] For the early Baptists their faith and their approach to the scriptures was set between rigid boundaries.

I am a Baptist, and hold the Distinctives that define a Baptist very close to my heart. One of these is "The Supremacy (or Sole Authority) and sufficiency of the Holy Scriptures in all matters of faith and practice".[8] What this means in practice is that the Baptist in his faith and in his conduct and in his understanding is governed by what the Bible says. Where the scriptures are silent he is silent. If there is not a very clear statement in scripture saying to do something in church or personal life, then he is not obliged to do it. This demands a high view of scripture and a readiness to submit to it. We do not wear vestments because we are not commanded to wear them. We do not have Bishops as we understand the local churches to be independent and Christ is the head of the church. We do not have priests because all our members are priests. But was one of our founding precepts, the one about not using the tool of reason in interpreting scriptures, correct?

So what does all this old dry church history mean? I am going to try and explain it by looking at some even older and dryer church history and also at my favourite passage of scripture, which I hope you will not find dry. That passage is John 8:3-11, which in the Authorised or King James Version of the Bible from 1611 says:

[3]*And the scribes and Pharisees brought unto him a woman taken in adultery; and when they had set her in the midst,* [4] *They say unto him, Master, this woman was taken in adultery, in the very act.* [5] *Now Moses in the law commanded us, that such should be stoned: but what sayest thou?* [6] *This they said, tempting him, that they*

---

[7] Hoad, Jack. *The Baptists. t*(London: Grace Publications Trust, 1986) ..., 278.
[8] Hoad. *The Baptist...,* 14.

might have to accuse him. But Jesus stooped down, and with his finger wrote on the ground, as though he heard them not. [7] So when they continued asking him, he lifted up himself, and said unto them, He that is without sin among you, let him first cast a stone at her. [8] And again he stooped down, and wrote on the ground. [9] And they which heard it, being convicted by their own conscience, went out one by one, beginning at the eldest, even unto the last: and Jesus was left alone, and the woman standing in the midst. [10] When Jesus had lifted up himself, and saw none but the woman, he said unto her, Woman, where are those thine accusers? hath no man condemned thee? [11] She said, No man, Lord. And Jesus said unto her, Neither do I condemn thee: go, and sin no more.

Imagine, if you can, that you are a pastor in the early church about 1800 years ago. A young man comes to you in deep distress for soul, why, because he has committed adultery. Sexual sin was treated far more seriously in the early church to the way it is today. He wants to know, can he find forgiveness, or will he forever live in the torment of Hell. Is his saviour able to be a saviour?

Well, as a good pastor you go to your Bible and it is an early copy of what we know as the *Codex Sinaiticus* (4th century), one of the most important hand-written ancient copies of the Greek Bible. You look it up and you have some bad news for him. Jesus never forgave a baptised believer of adultery. Immediately you remind me of the passage of the woman caught in adultery, but there is a problem. In modern English translations like the New International Version and the New Revised Standard Version this passage is simply missing. And it was missing in his New Testament 1800 years ago.

So you look further and see in Hebrews 10:26 *"For if we willfully persist in sin (wilfully sin NKJV) after having received the knowledge of the truth, there no longer remains a sacrifice for sins, [27] but a fearful prospect of judgment, and a fury of fire that will consume the adversaries*". Now this passage is probably meant to refer to "a certain [un-repairable] form of apostasy, adopted as a settled policy by [some] one who had once accepted Christianity and later, [just] as deliberately, decided to renounce it.".[9] Unfortunately it does not say that and many in the early church took it straight at face value. Young man, the scriptures offer you no hope, get used to the heat because it is hot where you are going. But then he remembers, this old Bible has at the back a book called the *Shepherd of Hermas. The Shepherd of Hermes* is a work of the second century that had such great authority that the leading early church fathers, Irenaeus and Tertullian considered it as scripture. This authority is why it is found in with the *Codex Sinaiticus*. He asks the young man, "how many times have you committed adultery"? Twice is the reply. Then he gives him the news, Son you are certainly going to burn.

The Shepherd of Hermas, the young only man's hope of escape, taught that there was forgiveness for sin after baptism but Gods grace could **cover only one sin** and not a second. About sin after baptism *The Shepherd* says *"For the Master sware by His own glory, as concerning His elect; that if, now that this day has been set as a limit, sin shall hereafter be committed, they shall not find salvation; for repentance for the righteous hath an end.* Tertullian thought that this was very lax and called Hermas, the *Shepherd of the Adulterers*.[10] I do not know if you have noticed, but it is unworkable, that is unless you don't have sinners in your congregation.

They had been interpreting the scriptures without sanctified reason and very soon had to start categorising sins into their seriousness to

---

[9] Bruce, F.F. *The Spreading Flame* (Eerdmans: Grand Rapids, 1958) 200.
[10] Bruce. *Spreading...*, 201.

offer some hope. This is where the idea of "deadly sins" came from. It came to a head in Rome under Callistus, Bishop of Rome from 217 to 222. He ruled "that sincere penitents **might** be readmitted to Christian communion even after adultery and fornication".[11] This was considered criminal laxity and for a time the church in Rome split under a second bishop. Fortunately for the adulterers you will have to help today, the view of Callistus won out. The Eastern Church held out much longer. John Chrysostom (c 347–407), the golden mouthed preacher, allowed for forgiveness of two or even three serious sins.[12] Going to a doctor for a second opinion I can understand, but going to a second theologian for an opinion on your adultery is ridiculous.

So, this great passage about Jesus recognizing sin for what it is, yet not condemning the sinner (which is why it is my favourite passage) and the hope of grace and mercy has been swept from under our feet. Or has it been? Is this part of God's word or not? For the Catholic Church, "the criterion of canonicity is acceptance into the Vulgate".[13] Acceptance by Jerome in his Latin translation would not be sufficient for the Protestants who require different criteria. Yet for many in the English speaking world, the sole criterion is simply whether it is part of the King James Bible.[14] Others, who are informed about the problems of authorship, are content to let the matter rest with church confessions.[15] For others,

---

[11] Bruce. *Spreading...*, 201

[12] Sermon of St John Chrysostom on the Epistle to the Colossians, Hom vii.

[13] Brown, Raymond E. *The Gospel According to John I-XII*, Anchor Bible Series Vol. 29. (New York: Doubleday, 1966) 336.

[14] Brown *Introduction...*, 336. It is difficult to say how much Brown oversimplifies. There is a reverence for the Authorised Version beyond which it deserves e.g. one Baptist college had a course on "A Defence of the KJV" (Louisiana Baptist University, 2000, 52) and the Gideons are still printing large quantities of the AV or New King James Version for distribution in the USA and Australia.

[15] "I am aware of the problems of authorship but as a Lutheran pastor I am obliged to believe that the letters are Paul's" (Eric Liebelt, Pers. Com. 2006).

the question is meaningless, or even an affront to Christianity as talk of any "preconceived notion of "inspiration" … will not bear examination when confronted with the facts".[16] They consider this book to be no different to any other.

Lets return to the story of the woman caught in adultery. Modern translations say something like "most ancient authorities lack 7.53—8.11" – and they are completely correct. But the story of this passage is far more complex than that because in some old hand copied New Testaments, it is found after John 7.36 or tacked on the end of John's gospel after 21.25 or even in a totally different book, after Luke 21.38. Some old manuscripts even mark the passage as doubtful and that is without considering the variations of text. Because of the textual changes and its different position, if it is present at all you cannot defend the claim that this wonderful passage was part of the original document as much as we want it to be.

Let us look more closely. Is it how we would expect Jesus to act? As one commentator said, "it rings true. It speaks to our condition".[17] The story of the woman caught in adultery is very old and over the long history of the church it was seen as an authentic story. It is most likely referred to by Papias (c. 70-155) when he "relate[d] another story of a woman, who was accused of many sins before the Lord, which is contained in the Gospel according to the Hebrews".[18] Here it is a different gospel again but we know of no other story of a woman taken to Jesus accused of sinning. The scholars tell us that most references to the woman caught in adultery are later and only by the western fathers centered around Rome. We find also that texts that contain our

---

[16] Guy, H.A. *The Gospel of Mark.* (Basingstoke: Macmillan, 1968) 2.

[17] Morris, Leon. *Commentary on the Gospel of John* (Eerdmans: Grand Rapids, 1971) 883.

[18] Eusebius. *Historia Ecclesiastica 3.39.17.* Papias was a companion of Polycarp who was a disciple of John.

passage are from the western church, not the east. Does this mean anything? Yes, in a church that believed that there was no forgiveness for sin after baptism, particularly in the Eastern Church, this story was seen as not been hard on adultery. It is reasonable to believe that after the church came to its senses, and read passages like Peters denial of Jesus and his later restitution, they did not want a genuine account of Jesus forgiving a sinner to be lost; they just were not agreed on where it should be put.

So what have we done? In the Hebrews passage we have seen the danger and bondage that can come about by not interpreting scripture critically, by not exposing it to reason and by not exposing it to light the gospel. We have then looked at the story of the woman caught in adultery and rationally thought about it in the way that the text has come to us today. We have asked hard questions about it. We have looked at it in the light of early church history and we have looked at it in the light of the gospel. We have thought critically about the Bible and the roof has not fallen in on us. Far from loosing this text through criticism, it comes back to us, fresh and with authority.

So I suppose the next question is, what are the limits of reason. Some would say that there are not many limits at all. The Roman Catholic Church has taught that the existence of God can be demonstrated by natural reason through what are called the *a posteriori* proofs.[19] These are arguments where only the existence of God can account for some aspect of the universe. Lutheran Theologians from Melanchthon (Luther's successor) up to Kierkegaard,[20] through the use of Aristotelian Philosophy could "prove" Creation *ex nihilo*, the resurrection of the body and the

---

[19]In 1835 Abbe Bautain, a prominent Catholic theologian of the time was forced to recant his belief that God is known by faith alone and acknowledge that his existence can be demonstrated by natural reason.

[20] He taught that a leap of faith was required to believe in God, not just a decision based on strong evidence.

trinity. Such exulted claims were made for reason and philosophy that it would appear that there was little remaining for revelation and faith.   If these claims were right they provide compelling ground for a belief in God and from which his nature could then be discovered. They would buttress faith, ultimately silencing doubts that assail in the face of suffering.

As recently as 1950 Pope Pius 12 pronounced in his encyclical *Humani Generis* that "human reason ... by its natural powers and light can in fact arrive at true and certain knowledge of one personal God who in his providence guards and directs the world and also the natural law infused into our souls by the creator." This was reiterated in Vatican 1 "that God, the beginning and end of all things, can be known with certitude by the natural light of human reason from created things"[21]

These proofs found their clearest expression in the five proofs of Thomas Aquinas[22].   Though they refused to die, the authority given to these arguments was destroyed by William of Ockham when he posed the question, "Does pushing back the cause-effect sequence to a prime mover really prove the existence of an Ultimate Being, namely the God of the Bible, or merely an adequate cause which might be a limited power or being but less than God himself".[23] A powerful being need not be an all powerful God.   This question aptly carries the name "Ockham's razor.". During the enlightenment Thomas' proofs were turned against the church as it was rightly pointed out that even if accepted, they said nothing, good or bad, about God's nature except that he designs.

---

[21]Schwarz H. *The Search for God* (Augsburg, Min. 1975) P. 58

[22]These are 1. Motion, God is the prime mover but not moved, 2. Causation, i.e. the cosmological argument where god is the uncaused cause, 3. Possibility and Necessity, God is absolutely independent, 4. Graduation of being, God is perfectly developed and 5. Governance of the world, i.e. the teleological argument, God gives the world its pattern.

[23]W. Menzies, *Apologetics*. (ICI: Brussels, 1988)

Ultimately reason alone will take you up what we would call "a dry creek bed", lots of promise of a good drink but ultimately leaving you dry and parched.

Many have spoken of a restlessness in man, such as a longing for truth, an awareness of his own finitude and a need for blessedness. Augustine in the opening of his *Confessions* reflected on man's relation to God, "thou hast made us for thyself and restless in our heart until it comes to rest in thee". These are all examples of *a priori* arguments where there is something about man that gives a clue to the existence of God. Other arguments in this category are the ontological, moral and aesthetic arguments. While many relate to the reasoning behind these arguments they are ultimately unverifiable.

In the *revelational* argument the traditional proofs are discarded and instead of man trying to prove that God exists, God himself proves his own existence. This is done through the proclamation of the Gospel and the experience is self authenticating. The diversity of the mystical religious experience show the danger of using the experience as the proof itself.

Ultimately the arguments from reason cannot substitute for, or validate faith. But reason, when it does not stand alone but allows the light of the gospel and life of faith to shine though it is a very powerful tool in seeing our God and understanding his word. There are four spiritual criteria that must be in place before anyone should even consider thinking critically about the scriptures[24]

1. **He must be born again**. In John 3:16 Jesus said to Nicodemus that except a man be born again he cannot see - can neither understand the nature of nor share the blessedness - of the Kingdom of God. This appears

---

[24] Ramm, Bernard. *Protestant Biblical Interpretation*. (Baker Book House: Grand Rapids,1982.) 13.

straightforward but look at the words of John A. T. Robinson, Bishop of Woolich in his controversial book "Honest to God". He said "I never seriously considered anything but being a parson ..... However I find myself a radical in matters theological, I belong to the once born rather than the twice born type".[25]

2. **He must have a passion to know Gods Word**, his enthusiasm breeding reverence and industry. Again this seems a basic requirement but look at what Rudolph Bultman, a leading German theologian of the last century said "It is impossible to use the electric light and wireless and to avail ourselves of modern medical and surgical discoveries and at the same time to believe in the New Testament world of spirits and miracles. We may think we can manage it in our lives, but to expect others to do so is to make the Christian faith unintelligible and unacceptable to the modern world.[26]

3. **The interpreter must have always a deep reverence for God**. Albert Schweitzer was held up as an example of a fine Christian man yet he approved of the writing of a man who said that "Jesus died a poor deluded fool".

4. **He must have an utter dependence on the Holy Spirit to guide and direct**. At this point we must not confuse inspiration with illumination which can only make men wise up to what is written in the scriptures, not beyond it. It will never communicate new truth.

Biblical interpretation is something the unregenerate does at his peril. Take the words of H. A. Guy in his "Gospel of Mark", "The term with which the man addressed Jesus, 'Holy one of God' is probably not a messianic title but indicates that he recognized something different or holy about Jesus. People who are not in full possession of their normal faculties often do have such second

---

[25] Robinson, John A.T. *Honest to God.* (SCM: London 1974) 27.

[26] Bultmann, Rudolf. New Testament and Mythology in H.W. Bartsch, (editor) *Kerygma & Myth.* (S.P.C.K. London,1984.) 5.

sight".[27] The book that this nonsense appears in was my textbook for A Level Religious Knowledge in the U.K. the syllabus of which he helped set. Young enquiring minds could easily be lead away from the truth of God. The words of James 3:1-2a should ever be before us; "Not many of you should become teachers, my brothers, for you know we are assuming the more accountability. And also, because we all make mistakes."

Conclusion

I hope this small work will encourage you to look at the scriptures with fresh eyes. To question it by all means, but with faith, not unbelief. God's word says many things that are hard to understand but we are encouraged to press in and mine for the gold that is there. Not in the sense of finding "deeper meanings" that are hidden to all but the initiated, but finding the truth that was intended to be found by all who will seek, truth that will enrich you and your hearers.

---

[27] Guy, H.A. *Gospel of Mark* (Macmillan, Basingstoke, 1971.) 56.

Works Cited

Bartsch, H.W. (editor) *Kerygma & Myth*. (S.P.C.K. London,1984).

Brown, Raymond E. *The Gospel According to John I-XII*. Anchor Bible Series Vol. 29. (New York: Doubleday, 1966).

Bruce, F.F. *The Spreading Flame*. (Eerdmans: Grand Rapids, 1958).

Estep, William R. *The Anabaptist Story*. (Grand Rapids: Eerdmans, 1975).

Friedenthal, Richard. *Luther*. Trans. John Nowell. (London: Weidenfeld and Nicolson, 1970).

Guy, H.A. *The Gospel of Mark*. (Basingstoke and London: Macmillan Education Limited, 1968).

Hoad, Jack. *The Baptist*. (London: Grace Publications Trust, 1986).

Morris, Leon. *Commentary on the Gospel of John*. (Grand Rapids: Eerdmans, 1971).

Ramm, Bernard. *Protestant Biblical Interpretatio.n* (Grand Rapids: Baker Book House, 1982).

Robinson John A.T. Honest to God. (SCM: London 1974).

Internet Sites

_____ *Shepherd of Hermas*. Early Christian Writings [online] URL http://web.archive.org/web/20080125125232/www.earlyc hristianwritings.com/text/shepherd-lightfoot.html Accessed 2 October 2009.

Eusebius. *Historia Ecclesiastica.* Christian Etherial Library [online] URL http://www.ccel.org/ccel/schaff/npnf201.html Accessed 27 Sept 2009.

Baptist Confession of 1689 URL http://www.reformedreader.org/ccc/1689lbc/english/Chapter01.htm Accessed 29 September 2009.

5 Decay, Bondage, Corruption and Our Future Glory

Background

My friend Fred Kornis and I were asked to speak at two conferences in the Philippines in December 2009. Because of the disastrous floods and landslides in the Philippines in 2009, The organisers asked me to abandon the subject they had chosen, "Thinking Critically about the Bible". Because the trauma the nation was experiencing, it was believed that the subject "Decay, Bondage, Corruption and Our Future Glory" was more appropriate. I was asked to prepare a 1 ½ hour address.

The first conference in Moncada, Tarlac City, was in English but if we added a translator which would be required at Barangay Paet, Alabael, Sarangani province southern Mindanao that was three hours! So I prepared a cut down version which kept to 90 minutes with translator. The organisers said "No, three hours is good. The people will say, we have walked 4 or 5 hours over these hills to get here and you only give us an hour and a half sermon, Pastor it is not fair"! (See the cover image) .I broke it into three one hour sessions.

The Spirit moved up in the hills in a powerful way. What impressed me was the way the lay workers so were so well organised and capable.

In Romans 8:17-27 we read *"17 and if children, then heirs, heirs of God and joint heirs with Christ—if, in fact, we suffer with him so that we may also be glorified with him.*

18I consider that the sufferings of this present time are not worth comparing with the glory about to be revealed to us. 19 For the creation waits with eager longing for the revealing of the children of God; 20 for the creation was subjected to futility, not of its own will but by the will of the one who subjected it, in hope 21 *that the creation itself will be set free from its bondage to decay and will obtain the freedom of the glory of the children of God. [22] We know that the whole creation has been **groaning** in labor pains until now; [23] and not only the creation, but we ourselves, who have the first fruits of the Spirit, **groan** inwardly while we wait for adoption, the redemption of our bodies. [24] For in hope we were saved. Now hope that is seen is not hope. For who hopes for what is seen? [25] But if we hope for what we do not see, we wait for it with patience.*

[26] *Likewise the Spirit helps us in our weakness; for we do not know how to pray as we ought, but that very Spirit intercedes with **sighs** too deep for words. [27] And God, who searches the heart, knows what is the mind of the Spirit, because the Spirit intercedes for the saints according to the will of God".*

When Pastor Noe called me to address these seminars here in the Philippines I was first asked to speak to you on the subject of *"How to Think Critically About the Bible"*. I worked hard on that talk because you deserve the best I could do and it was mostly done. I was really pleased with the way the message was shaping up, it would have tickled your intellect, perhaps, touched your spirit, perhaps, helped you look at the scriptures in a fresh way, I certainly hope so. While that is a subject I felt at home in, that is a subject for happier days. Typhoon Kestana has intervened and so Pastor Noe then asked me to prepare, instead, a message based on Romans 8:18-27, the passage we have just read. He wanted me to look particularly at the theme of *Decay* and *Bondage* and *Corruption*. I had to admit that I agreed with him but I have gone back one extra verse to 17 which will put our pain into perspective. Despite the study I have done, and I have done more than most, I feel very inadequate to share this subject with you. I have never seen or experienced the pain many of you have, so what can I have to say to you? It is you who should be ministering to me. While I had not studied or read much on the subject of decay, bondage and corruption, I knew where to go for research. A lot of what I am going to say I have drawn from sermons by the prince of British preachers, Dr Martin Lloyd-Jones. You will see a number of quotations from him in the footnotes but I have not followed him blindly.

So, I am a businessman from Australia, what would I know of pain, and what would our blessed nation know of natural disaster. Just like the Philippines we are not immune and they seem to be getting worse. Just this year on Saturday, February 7th we experienced extreme bushfire-weather conditions, which resulted in 400 fires in the state of Victoria. That day saw the highest ever loss of life from a bushfire when 173 people died and 414 were injured. It is known in Australia as "Black Saturday". Over 2000 homes were destroyed and 450,000 hectares were burnt. At one stage the fire storm was travelling at 120 km per hour. Up in my home state of Queensland, when the south of Australia was burning, half of my state was affected by floods. The total area of Queensland is 1,734,000 square kilometres which means that over 800,000 square km were affected. To get this in perspective, the total area of the Philippines is 300,000 sq kilometres! But my town never floods and never burns and never has strong winds and these disasters were a long way from home.[28] So, while our nation knows the pain of natural disaster, I have been blessed to avoid it. But I have not been able to avoid other sorts of pain and I know what it is like to have an ache so deep in my heart that nothing can fill it.

The sorrow of this present world is summed in this passage. Here **creation groans**, **we groan** and **the Spirit himself groans**. Here we see ever increasing depths of anguish, just like an orchestra building up to a climax with level upon level of suffering. It is all the same Greek root. The *Theological Dictionary of the New Testament* says of this word "*Sighing takes place by reason of a condition of oppression under which man suffers and from which*

---

[28] In January 2011 my valley would be hit by an "inland tsunami", something unprecedented in Australia's known history. Many died and the destruction was beyond belief.

he longs to be free because it is not in accord with his nature, expectations, or hopes".[29] Do you, like me, long to be free of the oppression of this world. Do you feel its pain, its disappointments and its heartbreaks? As pastors you know that this oppression can be too much to bear as not only must you carry your own pain, but the Lord has called you to carry the burden of the oppressed that call you their shepherd.

Verse 18 starts "For I consider" or "I reckon" as the English King James version says. This great passage of the coming redemption of the totality of God's creation, not just individual Christians, starts with the words "for I reckon". In Australia we frequently use the saying "I reckon" but what we are really saying is "my opinion is this or that". Paul is saying something very different. "The word 'reckon' means that you arrive at a conclusion, at a deduction, by a process of logical thinking".[30] Paul is not offering some very general message of hope to make you feel good. What Paul is about to say is based on what he has just said, and he has said some very remarkable things.

The eighth chapter of Romans is probably the greatest of all Paul's writings. This chapter shows how we, as Christians, can have complete assurance of our salvation. By the time we have reached verses 17 to 27 we should hade no doubt that we are the sons of God. Look at what Paul says - in **verses 1 to 3**, there is no condemnation for the believer. The claim of God's Law on us and the penalty for breaking it have been set aside. Any claim it may have had on us has been satisfied by Christ's sacrifice. In **verses 4 to 6**, our minds are set on the ways of the Spirit and we are free to walk in them because we are rid of the condemnation of the law.

---

[29]G. Kittel, G. W. Bromiley and G. Friedrich, Ed. *Theological dictionary of the New Testament.* 1964-c1976. Vols. 5-9 edited by Gerhard Friedrich. Vol. 10 compiled by Ronald Pitkin. (electronic ed.) . Eerdmans: Grand Rapids, MI.
[30] Lloyd-Jones, D. Martin. *Romans, Exposition of Chapter 8:17-39, The Final Perseverance of the Saints.* (Edinbrough: Banner of Truth, 1975) 23.

In **verses 7 and 8**, Paul assures us that the very fact that our mind is set on spiritual things is evidence that we are no longer God's enemy. In **verses 9 to 11** we find that we belong to God. The evidence of this is that God's Spirit which raised Jesus from the dead has raised us and actually lives in us also. In **verses 12 to 14** we see that the evidence that God's Spirit is leading us is that we now act with righteousness. **In verses 15 to 16** Paul says that there is something within us that stirs our heart to call God our Father and to know with certainty that we are his sons.

"Are you a Christian", Paul might be asking? He simply would not accept the answers, "I hope so", or "I would like to think so", or "probably I am". Nothing could be further from his understanding of our faith. Did you see the strength of the encounter with God Paul was describing? There should be no uncertainty when we come to this. Every part of our life, our mind, our actions our desires and our interaction with the Spirit must cry out that we are sons of God.

It has all been good up to **verse 17** when we are introduced to something we do not want to hear. We are joint heirs with our saviour, that is good, that is very good. We are united with Jesus in our salvation. What we do not want to hear is that we suffer with him so that we may be glorified with him. Of course we want the glory, but we do not like the cost. The cost is suffering. As if all the evidences above were not enough to prove that we are God's sons, Paul gives another. Our trials and suffering give the final evidence that we will be glorified with Jesus, the man of sorrows who was acquainted with grief. I have been asked to look at *Decay* and *Bondage* and *Corruption* but here it is partnered with glorification – "*and if children, then heirs, heirs of God and joint heirs with Christ—if, in fact, we suffer with him so that we may also be glorified with him*" We suffer with him, but we inherit with him and in due time we will be glorified in him.

In the beginning God created man with a degree of glory. Our forefather Adam was made in God's image and likeness. He was granted dominion over every living thing and the whole of creation was his to subdue (Gen 1:28-31). There was nothing in God's creation that was not there for his benefit. Despite this glory being upon Adam and his wife, they both fell into temptation and sin and this resulted a world that refuses to be subdued. Earlier in Romans, Paul had told them (3:23) that *all have sinned and fall short of the glory of God*. You and I were never meant to fall short of God's glory and were never meant to live in a world of decay and bondage and corruption. We were never meant to live in a world where creation is our master. Certainly man is attempting to subdue the world, and the command to Adam to bring this world under control is as valid to God's fallen creation as it was Him. But many of the things that he discovered soon get so twisted because of man's sin they can even become mankind's destruction - nuclear power or nuclear bombs, disease control or germ warfare, genetic based treatments or weapons that can target a single race, powerful fertilizers or powerful bombs. "creation is too vast, too big for him; and man has become the victim of the creation of which he was originally appointed lord and controller. That is part of the glory which has been lost as a result of sin"[31]. Mankind wanted to be like God by gaining the knowledge **of** good and evil but in the end lost his glory and gained instead knowledge **for** good and evil. Did man, and I mean unredeemed man, loose all of his glory in the fall, it is debated. Man still remained in God's image – remember the time they tried to trap Jesus about whether it was right to pay the temple tax? He asked for a coin. "Whose image is on it"? "Caesar's" they said. Then give to Caesar what is Caesar's and to God what is God's (Matt 22:17-22). You are in God's image and should be given to him, but possessing some of God's glory is another matter. I would say no, some would say yes

---

[31] Lloyd-Jones, *Romans, 8:17-39...*, 6.

but very damaged.

It is not just lifeless creation that is undergoing decay, bondage and corruption but mankind also who was the peak of our father's labours. When he looked on creation he said, "it was good" (Gen. 1:25) but it was not perfect. After he made man God looked upon Adam and Eve and his creation he said it was "very good" (Gen. 1:31). God's glory was revealed in man in his perfection before the fall, in a body without disease and without pain and a spirit that spoke to God as a friend speaks to a friend. Our very bodies now are our disgrace. Paul refers to them as "the body of our humiliation" (Phil. 3:21). It is a body of decay and bondage and corruption from which God's glory had departed from every part, spirit soul and body. There is a restlessness about man who is always striving for more wealth, more honour, more power. For many, this is probably no more than some deep seated recognition of what we were destined for. But unredeemed man can not return to it, he can never recapture it. He lost whatever glory he had and was driven from the garden and an angel with a flaming sword guarded its entry to forbid their return.

When we talk about the salvation that is only found in Christ, we can only start to grasp its meaning when we look at where we have come from, when we understand how far we have fallen. Our brother Fred, as an evangelist, proclaims and re-proclaims the gospel, the gracious promise of forgiveness in Christ Jesus. But when he does this, he knows that this is not all there is to the gospel. God does not forgive us and leave us unchanged but starts to recreate his glory in us. He gives us a new heart, he transforms our mind, he transforms our actions but does all this in a body subject to decay and bondage and corruption, a body that has come from dust and will returned to dust. As our body sees corruption has the evil one finally succeeded in the end?

Glorification, not the grave is the ultimate goal of salvation.

Lloyd-Jones described this goal saying "Glorification is the ultimate end and goal of salvation; and we must never stop short of it. We must never think of our Christian position as merely one of being forgiven".[32] Salvation that is less than the full restoration of God's creation back to what it was is not full salvation. This would be wonderful if that is what salvation is, a world without bondage and corruption, a return to what was. But it is more! There was no defect in mankind before the fall but he was in a state of innocence, without the knowledge of good and evil. In their perfection and innocence they fell short of full glorification. Of course there was room for development and, if they remained faithful, they would have achieved it as glorification was the ultimate end of man. The promise of the gospel is that Christ's own are not just redeemed from decay but gain far more. They will share something of the glory of our dear Lord and saviour.

Paul's argument up to verse 17 has been that we are free from the tyranny of sin because we have died with Christ. We are now dead to sin and to the law. But sin intrudes, we deceive ourselves if we say it doesn't, but it doesn't have dominion over us. We are saved and secure but we are not yet glorified. But what is this "glorification"? Fallen humanity, as I have said has glimpses of what he has lost, but we have glimpses of what we will gain! I do not understand what this glory is but we are given a foretaste of what is install for us. When we have experienced the intimacy of God's Spirits we have tasted the firstfruits (or deposit) of our inheritance (8:23). Paul describes it in 2 Corinthians 3:18 *"But we all, with open face beholding as in a glass the glory of the Lord, are changed into the same image from glory to glory, even as by the Spirit of the Lord"*. We do not need to know in detail what this glory is, but what glimpses we see of it are enough to make us long for it. As Paul says we *"rejoice in hope of the glory of God"*

---

[32] Lloyd-Jones, *Romans, 8:17-39...*, 4.

(Rom. 5:2).

At the moment we are like Moses who was allowed to see the Promised Land from afar off. Our bodies know only decay, bondage and corruption and the constant battle with sin as we strive to be transformed into God's image. Yet for all that, we see our ultimate glorification in the distance. How can I know these things to be true? I said it in the introduction, Are you led by the Spirit? What sort of things does he lead you to? You cannot be a Christian and not know the leading of the Holy Spirit. Does God's Spirit talk to your spirit to convince to you that you are our Heavenly Father's child? Not all who know the leading of God's Spirit experience the witness of the spirit. You cannot say that because you cannot name your heavenly father as your father, without any doubt, that you are not a Christian. Many Christians fight with having the certainty of their salvation. But if as Christians you suffer that is certain evidence that you are God's child. "As he suffered so shall we. So if we are suffering because of our relationship to him it is an absolute proof of our relationship to him".[33]

For the apostles, suffering and glory go hand in hand. These are opposites yet they are inseparable. In John chapter 15 and 17 the great sorrow of Christ's passion and the sorrow of his disciples end in their joy being complete, 17:24. Earlier in Romans 5:1 and 2 it is unmistakable *"Therefore being justified by faith, we have peace with God through our Lord Jesus Christ: [2]By whom also we have access by faith into this grace wherein we stand, and rejoice in hope of the glory of God. [3]And not only so, but we glory in tribulations also: knowing that tribulation worketh patience"*. For Paul It is equally clear in 2 Corinthians 4:17. *"For our light affliction, which is but for a moment, worketh for us a far more exceeding and eternal weight of glory"*. Two verses further on in

---

[33] Lloyd-Jones, *Romans, 8:17-39...*, 10

5:1 he says *"For we know that if our earthly house of this tabernacle were dissolved, we have a building of God, an house not made with hands, eternal in the heavens"*. Christ in you is the hope of Glory so says Colossians 1:27 but, make no mistake, this hope of Glory is rooted in suffering. Three verses earlier Paul had said *"Who now rejoice in my sufferings for you, and fill up that which is behind of the afflictions of Christ in my flesh for his body's sake, which is the church: ²⁵Whereof I am made a minister"*. Again it is clear in 2 Timothy 2:12 *If we suffer, we shall also reign with him*

My dear friends, many of you who have suffered so much, yet you must not stumble at this. You must never think "how can I be a child of God if I am suffering". It is the clear teaching of our Lord and his apostles that you will surely suffer. The Glory that has been promised to us is only approached through decay and bondage and corruption! You don't understand this? Neither do I. The passage Pastor Noe has asked me to speak about explains this connection between corruption and the glory to come. Paul could have just made the connection between suffering and glorification and moved on to the next subject but like a pastor he stays with this difficult subject as he wants to help. He has a point to make. Christians are aware of their glorification but it is easy to forget that this wayward creation is also going to be glorified, and its deliverance is as certain as ours.

Creation Groans

In verse 20, Paul says that the world is subjected to "vanity" or "futility". This could be described as something that is not fulfilling its function. How could it! Paul goes on to say that creation is in a state of corruption, by that he means putrefaction, like decaying meat. It is offensive, and it cannot rid itself of this corruption because it is in bondage to it (8:21). That is why creation is ultimately futile. There is change and decay in everything we see. Creation was "made subject" to vanity which means that it wasn't always that way but a single, unrepeatable, definite act in the past (aorist tense) changed everything. This was not its own doing - *not of its own will but by the will of the one who subjected it.*

It wasn't man who bought this world into corruption. He has been trying his hardest to do the very opposite, to bring it under control. Nor was it the evil one. It was God himself who caused the perfect creation of his to be subject to decay, bondage and corruption. But it was subjected *in hope,* and it is not the Devils plan to ever give any hope of restoration. You read this in Genesis 3 14-19. – *cursed is the ground for your sake.* The creation was cursed because of man's sin. God's creation is incredible – certainly it is, but we are not looking at creation as it was or was intended to be. There were not meant to be thorns or soul destroying labour or floods or earthquakes. The Genesis account tells us of how mankind sinned willingly and must endure the consequence, but nature became subject to corruption unwillingly. The lord of creation fell, and everything that was under him fell along with him.

At the moment we live in a world that is *futile.* The New English Bible gives us a very clear understanding of what is happening in verse 22, *"Up to the present, we know, the whole created universe groans in all its parts as if in the pangs of childbirth".* Paul is using poetic language. He is picturing the world in all its troubles as if it trying to give birth to something better. But it never does, spring is always followed by summer which quickly turns into autumn and the back again to winter – at least in Australia. I think you only have wet and dry season. It is no better than man, sensing that there is something better and striving for it but never able to achieve it.

But there is hope for creation as it was *subjected in hope.* The hope for God's creation lies in only one thing, and that is the character of God as saviour. "God's glory and Gods honour prohibit his leaving the world the way it is"[34]. When Paul described this world as groaning in labour pains, of it suffering *in hope* there was also the promise of this world's redemption. When man was cursed there was the promise of a deliverer. In Genesis 3:15 we read the first promise of the gospel "*and I will put enmity between thee and the woman, and between thy seed and her seed; it shall bruise thy head, and thou shalt bruise his heel*". But if God was promising hope of a redeemer to mankind it must also extend to the creation subject to corruption. When man is restored to his former glory and taken beyond to share in Christ's glory it will be in a world that does not produce thorns and require soul destroying labour. The coming glory of verse 17 is going to extend to a world, no longer "groaning". Lord hasten that day.

Humanity Groans

Mankind is always trying to bring around change, to bring, if not perfection, at least some order to this chaotic world. There have been times when it looks as if order was to going break out, as in the aftermath of World War 1, the war to end all wars. The League of Nations was founded, a forum where differences could be talked out over a table rather than on a battlefield. Yet, only twenty years later, the world was deep in an even greater cataclysm and with it came a sense of despair from which we have not recovered. Our great period of unprecedented financial boom has been followed by the world financial crisis. As I said earlier, there is a sense that things are not meant to be this way. But mankind cannot make it happen. There is no hope for creation and so we also groan, waiting for the adoption, the redemption of our bodies, where our bodies will no longer be suspect to bondage corruption and decay, but bodies that are glorified. No wonder we groan. It is not just

---

[34] Lloyd-Jones, *Romans, 8:17-39..., 57.*

the bondage of corruption and decay that we must endure on a daily basis that makes us groan, and that would be enough, but it is seeing far off that future glory, the glory of Christ which we will share. Paul says to those who are weighed down by this pressure – the sufferings of this present time are not worthy to be compared with the glory that will be revealed in us. "Nature, inanimate nature has some awareness of this, so how much more should we have it".[35]

We are given a glimpse of the glory that will be ours when we look at Christ's glory. We are glorified with him. In the story of the Mount of Transfiguration in Luke 9:28-31 we read *"Jesus took with him Peter and John and James, and went up on the mountain to pray. [29] And while he was praying, the appearance of his face changed, and his clothes became dazzling white. [30]Suddenly they saw two men, Moses and Elijah, talking to him. [31] They appeared in glory and were speaking of his departure, which he was about to accomplish at Jerusalem"*. For a short moment the disciples glimpsed the glory that we will share with Jesus. But did you see that it was shared? Moses and Elijah also appeared in glory. You might say to me, "What would you expect, they were great men, and they "deserved" it".

Peter was an eyewitness of Christ's glory and when he knew his death would occur soon he wrote to ordinary believers like you and me to reinforce certain things he had been teaching them (2 Peter 1:15-18). He told them *"Therefore I intend to keep on reminding you of these things, though you know them already and are established in the truth that has come to you. [13] I think it right, as long as I am in this body, to refresh your memory, [14]since I know that my death will come soon, as indeed our Lord Jesus Christ has made clear to me. [15]And I will make every effort so that after my*

[35] Lloyd-Jones, *Romans, 8:17-39...*, 61.

departure you may be able at any time to recall these things. I have come here today to do no more than Peter, to refresh your memory about what you already know. What are we reminding you of? Peter goes on to say *"For we did not follow cleverly devised myths when we made known to you the power and coming of our Lord Jesus Christ, but we had been eyewitnesses of his majesty. ¹⁷For he received honour and glory from God the Father when that voice was conveyed to him by the Majestic Glory, saying, "This is my Son, my Beloved, with whom I am well pleased." ¹⁸ We ourselves heard this voice come from heaven, while we were with him on the holy mountain"*. Peter is saying "Keep your focus". This world at times is awful but God allowed us to see the glory that Jesus has and we will be glorified with him.

But after speaking of the glory of our dear Lord that shone like the sun, the glory that will be ours Peter puts our present state into perspective *¹⁹So we have the prophetic message more fully confirmed. You will do well to be attentive to this as to a lamp shining in a dark place, until the day dawns and the morning star rises in your hearts.* Our life in this world of bondage, corruption and decay can only be compared to a lamp shining in a dark place. In the midst of the sorrows and joys that this world brings, we are still to let what glory we now have from God already shine in this dark world. And make no mistake as our Heavenly Father creates the image of his son in us, there should be a measure of glory, veiled, dim, but present just the same.

Future glory which will be poured out on us without measure, and present suffering, often also seemingly without measure, remain handmaidens. Paul knew something of the glory that Jesus has. He encountered it on the road to Damascus (Acts 9:3-5) *"a light from heaven flashed around him. ⁴He fell to the ground and heard a voice saying to him, "Saul, Saul, why do you persecute me?" ⁵He asked, "Who are you, Lord?" The reply came, "I am Jesus, whom you are persecuting".* Paul describes that glory as *"brighter than the sun, shining around me and my companions"* (Acts 26:13) but just a short time later when he was blind and praying in Damascus we read that God told Ananias *I myself will show him how much he must suffer for the sake of my name* (Acts 9:16). Future glory and present pain have always gone hand in hand. Jesus has promised that we *"will shine like the sun in the kingdom of their Father"* (Matt 13:43), the very same language that is used of himself. But the suffering is his suffering also

So humanity, like the creation groans and will continue to groan until God's glory is revealed in us. Lord don't you care? He cares more than you know.

The Spirit Groans

*"Likewise the Spirit helps us in our weakness; for we do not know how to pray as we ought, but that very Spirit intercedes with **sighs** too deep for words"*. Creation is groaning, we are groaning and now the Spirit groans. Does it all get too much for you? Have the problems of this world been too much for you? Have you ever been in a situation where you simply do not know what to ask of the Lord? You are not the first one. Have you ever prayed prayers that should not have been uttered? Paul did this – you know the story of the thorn in his flesh. Jesus had to face this temptation. In John 12:27 we read *"Now my soul is troubled. And what should I say—'Father, save me from this hour'? No, it is for this reason that I have come to this hour"*. The writer of Hebrews In chapter 5 verses 5 to 8 gives a commentary on this passage *"In the days of his flesh, Jesus offered up prayers and supplications, with loud cries and tears, to the one who was able to save him from death, and he was heard because of his reverent submission. [8]Although he was a Son, he learned obedience through what he suffered"*. The anguish of his heart made him a better high priest and the anguish of your heart, I am afraid to say, will make you a better pastor.

I have observed over the years that ministers often rush in, claim the blood of Jesus, rebuke the Devil, reject the problem and quote the right bible verses. I have also observed that often nothing changes. My dear friends, it is alright to say, "This pain is beyond me, I don't know what to do, I don't know what Jesus would have me do". My friend, do not lie to God or to your members or too yourself. This passage says that there are problems that are simply too big for you. There are times when all the eloquence in prayer that you have learned is worth nothing. You know that you can go into God's presence but you have nothing to say because you do not know what to say. The more readily you can admit it, the better pastor you will be. Why? Because it is then that you have to rely completely on God's Spirit.

I started by reminding you of the proofs that Paul gave so we can know we are a Children of God and here is another. We know we are God's child when the Spirit helps us in our times of deepest need. Remember what it says, "The Spirit himself helps" as one translation puts it, not some guardian angel. If you want to understand, in part, the roll of the Spirit look in Job 9:32-35 where he complains about God to his three miserable comforters ."[3] *For he is not a mortal, as I am, that I might answer him, that we should come to trial together.[33]There is no umpire[36] between us, who might lay his hand on us both. [34]If he would take his rod away from me, and not let dread of him terrify me,[35]then I would speak without fear of him ,for I know I am not what I am thought to be".* But by 16:19 Job is daring to think such an umpire might exist [19] *Even now, in fact, my witness is in heaven, and he that vouches for me is on high.[20]My friends scorn me; my eye pours out tears to God,[21]that he would maintain the right of a mortal with God, as one does for a neighbor".* Job never saw his defender, but what he hopes for – you know. When God seems against you there is someone to stand between you both, someone who will plead your case. There is someone to put a hand on both your shoulders.

---

[36] Another reading is "*Would that there were an umpire*".

The Spirit groans, that is what the text says but some will not accept this. It can't be possible they say. Certainly Jesus groaned but his divinity was clothed in frail human flesh. Even the great Lloyd-Jones says it cannot be the Spirit groaning. The Spirit is part of the Godhead so he knows everything, how can he be short of words? The Spirit is our "advocate and his role is to put words into the man's mouth, to tell him what to say"[37] so they say. We are moved, our emotions are moved by the Spirit producing this emotion within us. But this will not do! It is not what the text says for a start.

The Almighty has been described as *impassible* from the Latin meaning "without passions"[38] and some have seen in this a God without moral character.[39] The term is generally understood now to refer simply to the belief that God is incapable of being acted on by anything stronger than himself, a confirmation of his omnipotence and perfection. But the Godhead is far from being without passion, it is consumed with it.[40] The parable of the Prodigal Son shows the Father rejoicing at the repentance of sinners while suffering on account of the sin of man and his unrequited love to man. There is little consolation in a God who only sympathises with us. We have already mentioned how Christians are often called to suffer with Christ but this is only one side of the picture. True consolation comes when we view the other side of the scene where we see the Lord of Glory who suffers when even the least of those who have put their trust in Him, suffer.

This entering into our suffering can be seen also through the

---

[37] Lloyd-Jones, *Romans, 8:17-39…, 136.*

[38] e.g Article 1 of the 39 Articles of the Church of England.

[39] This Platonic view came into the church through the early church fathers.

[40] See Gen 6:6; 1 Sam 15:11, 15:23 (cf. 2 Sam 24.16; Mal 3:6) John 12:23-24, 27-28, 13:31-31, 17:1,

ministry of the Holy Spirit who intercedes for us when we are so deeply troubled that we do not know how or what to pray. Far from instructing us, as a school teacher might, he enters right into the intensity of our emotions praying to the Father as we only wished we could (Rom 8:26). We are called to follow Christ and bear the *cross of Christ*, Lk 14:27 and this can involves "walking in the same way as Christ walked in the humble form of a servant - needy, forsaken, mocked not loving worldliness .... to walk alone"[41] But we have also been called to bear the *yoke of Christ*, Matt 11.30. As the young oxen is yoked to the older experienced animal and the pair share the same burden, so are we to be yoked to Christ.

It was this present world that Christ loved - a world full of decay, bondage and corruption and it was for this corrupt world he suffered. The suffering of Christ with us must therefore carry with it a logical progression and that is, we also share in the sufferings and judgements that befall our community, nation and world. His body must continue that same love and, as it were, complete the sufferings of Christ. God would "rather risk that the danger of their love may grow cold in the midst of judgements than the much greater danger that in their public preservation they will lose their love for their guilty brothers and sisters who are bought under judgement, and that they finally will proudly say, "I am not as they are"[42] Through this type of suffering the Christian can stand with the impenitent in their time of shame and associate with them and their guilt. Through experiencing the guilt of the community, confession of its sin (Dan 9:3-6) and practical demonstrations of God's love his kingdom will be advanced.

---

[41]Kierkegaard S. The Gospel of Suffering (Augsburg, Minneapolis, 1948) 12.
[42]Thielicke H. *Out of the Depths* (Eerdmans, Grand Rapids, 1962) 49.

Living with Bondage Decay and Corruption

How should a child of God live in this world with its bondage, decay and corruption? How should we react to all the troubles of this world that we encounter? Above everything it should be lived with our future glory in view but how do you do this?

Firstly: We should never be surprised at the fact of this corruption. You want to be united in fellowship with Christ in his glory but you can't do this without being in the fellowship of his suffering.

Secondly: Paul was writing to the Roman Christians who were surprised and deeply disappointed that life was not easy. Not only should we not be surprised but we are not meant to be shaken either. Christian witness in adversity was one of the strongest means of bringing unbelievers to faith. It is fairly obvious that if we do not deal well with this world's bondage corruption and decay we will hurt the gospel. Nothing will shake unbelievers more than to see a believer rise above the situation. I am reminded of the first persecution of Christians in Rome.

In July 64, two years after the end of Acts, a great fire destroyed much of Rome affecting 10 of its 14 areas. Nero was blamed for this even by the contemporary historians (Suetonius, Pliny the Elder, and Dio Cassius). In an attempt to deflect the blame, Nero accused the Christians of this and the first persecution begun. Tacitus wrote of this in his Annals: *Accordingly, an arrest was first made of all who confessed; then, upon their information, an immense multitude was convicted, not so much of the crime of arson, as of hatred of the human race. Mockery of every sort was added to their deaths, Covered with the skins of beasts, they were torn by dogs and perished, or were nailed to crosses, or were doomed to the flames. These served to illuminate the night when daylight failed. Nero had thrown open his gardens for the spectacle, and was exhibiting a show in the circus, while he mingled with the people in the dress of a charioteer. Hence even for criminals who deserved extreme and exemplary punishment, there arose a feeling of compassion; for it was not, as it seemed for the public good, but to glut one man's cruelty that they were being destroyed.[43]*

Australia was troubled for many years by the "prosperity gospel". Its preachers claimed that you could speak your prosperity into existence by making a positive confession. Paul knows nothing of this.

Thirdly: A child of God must never question whether he is a Christian because he is suffering. Brother Fred (Kornis) will never preach to the unbelievers – come to Jesus and all your problems will be over.

Fourthly: It would be easy to doubt God's love when this world's calamities come upon us. I love the story about Martin Luther, when he was hidden away from the Pope by his protectors in the tower in the Wartburg castle in Germany. There he translated the Bible into German. One night apparently the devil appeared to him and told him he would never succeed. Luther picked up the inkpot and threw it at him and the ink stain is still on the wall in his room almost 500 years later. When the evil one whispers in your heart that your suffering is proof that God does not love you, what are you going to throw at him? What you could throw back at him is that this trouble is proof that you are loved and that when he is finally cast into the lake of fire, you will be glorified with Christ. Our suffering should never lead us to think we are not Christians.

Fifthly: Don't ever think that this problem is too big for God.

---

[43] XV. 44.5-8

Never think it was too big for him to stop and it is now too big for
him to fix it. If you believe, as Paul has been teaching, that God
has the power, it easy to develop a grudge against our dear Lord
and Saviour. You must never do this. In Christian circles we hear
the word "faith" spoken a lot, and this faith can sometimes be said
to manipulate God, he must respond to our faith – it is a spiritual
law – if you have faith as a grain of mustard seed etc. But the
word I prefer is "trust". We can have faith in faith itself only to
find that God will not be manipulated. But trust is a different
matter. As Job said (13:15) *Though he slay me, yet will I trust him.*

Sixthly: There is no promise that your life was going to be easy.
One of our Australian Prime Ministers said something that is now
very often quoted in Australia – "life wasn't meant to be easy".
There is only one promise made to you in this world of bondage,
decay and corruption, and this is not of an easy life and riches in
this world. You are promised that if you are trusting Jesus your
sins are forgiven. And if your sins are forgiven, you will be
glorified with Christ. Karl Marks called religion the opiate of the
masses. He claimed that there is some general kind of comfort
offered through a life of faith. Nothing could be further from what
Paul is saying. This is a world of wars and rumours of wars, and
where evil men and impostors will go from bad to worse,
deceiving and being deceived (2 Tim 3:13). "There is nothing to
anticipate in this world but suffering and trials in various shapes
and forms".[44]

Seventhly: There is no command to this world to reform this world
and make it heaven on earth. We must be law abiding (Rom 13).
But more than that, in our society we have a opportunity, and with
the opportunity, the responsibility to participate. There is no all
powerful emperor. Even in the Philippines your politicians must

[44] Lloyd-Jones, *Romans, 8:17-39…,18*

stand for election and you have a say. You can participate at a local level. You can be involved in the passing of laws through lobbying your politicians. In our society this is what being subject to the governing authorities means. But for all that, as another of our Prime Ministers very wisely said, "you cannot legislate righteousness". Good laws with an honest police force and magistrates and an appropriate penal system will restrain some overt sin but that does not equate to righteousness. It will never eliminate wickedness. Christianity is not meant to be an overreaching influence to reform a lost and troubled world by exercising a moral influence. It is about turning sinners into saints one at a time. It will never abolish the causes of suffering.

Eightly: We do not simply resign ourselves to what we see and experience. We do not deny the pain but fully acknowledge it. But in acknowledging it we must look beyond it. When we look beyond this world's corruption, bondage and decay we see our future glory. If we really grasp this, we become "more than conquerors" in this world. As Romans 8:37-39 says *"No, in all these things we are more than conquerors through him who loved us. [38]For I am convinced that neither death nor life, neither angels nor demons, neither the present nor the future, nor any powers, [39] neither height nor depth, nor anything else in all creation, will be able to separate us from the love of God that is in Christ Jesus our Lord"*. This is not resignation.

We have a saying in Australia, "he is so heavenly minded that he is no earthly use". Having a mindset that sees only the coming glory and stoically endures this world's bondage, decay and corruption is not a Christian attitude either. The command to Adam was to subdue the earth (Gen 1:28). In many areas man has either subdued or has the power to subdue the scourges that afflict this world. It is estimated that smallpox killed somewhere between

300-500 million people during the 20th century. In December 1979 the World Health Organisation officially declared the disease eradicated. Plagues that killed one third of Europe are unheard of. How many of us here would not be alive if it was not for the advances in medicine. There has never been a time when the earth needed subduing more than now. Have you noticed that the climate is changing? While our icecaps melt, some are still in denial. It seems to me that there is no denying climate change, only how much is caused by men. We talk about our bodies being the temple of the Holy Spirit and we should treat it accordingly, but this poor world which our Lord declared to be very good is treated little better than a toilet. Of particular concern to the Philippines is probably illegal logging and the lack of flood mitigation measures. You can fix these if you have the will!

Ninthly: If we are overwhelmed by events, if we think that God has stopped loving us, that he is unfair, that the problem is too big then we are not thinking clearly. I remind you of what I said in the beginning and I read Rom 8:18 to you again *"For I reckon that the sufferings of this present time are not worthy to be compared with the glory which shall be revealed in us"*. It is down to that word "reckon" - I said "The word 'reckon' means that you arrive at a conclusion, at a deduction, by a process of logical thinking"[45]. I quote Lloyd-Jones again "The business of preaching is not merely to make the hearer feel a little happier while he is listening or while he is singing particular hymns; it is not meant to be a way of producing an atmosphere of comfort. If I do that I am a quack (an unqualified and incompetent doctor) and I am a very false friend indeed. No, The business of preaching is to teach you to think"[46].

Finally: Whatever I have said before only applies to Christians. There is no future glory for those outside of Christ. My friend's

[45] Lloyd-Jones, *Romans, 8:17-39...*, 23.
[46] Lloyd-Jones, *Romans, 8:17-39...*,24.

we know that there is a heaven to win but my Australian society does not want to hear that there is a hell to shun. We are too sophisticated to believe in that old myth. They will not consider that the troubles of this world are but a foretaste of the troubles to come. The words of an evangelist like Fred will fall flat on the ground with most in Australia.

Make no mistake; there is no comfort for those who remain outside of Christ in the preaching of the gospel. Our future glory comes only through confronting our own corruption caused by sin. It is critical that you do the work of an evangelist.

Conclusion

When our Lord was on this earth he did many miracles, or signs as John calls them. Consider his seven signs:

Reference	Event	Jesus, the master of
2:1-11	Water into wine	Quality – He made a change that normally takes months
4:46-54	Healing nobleman's son	Distance – The boy was 20 miles away
5:1-9	Healing of the impotent man	Time - afflicted for 38 years
6:1-14	Feeding the five thousand	Quantity
6:16-21	Walking on water	Natural law
9:1-12	Healing of the man born blind	Misfortune
11:1-46	The raising of Lazarus	Death

His miracles were pointers to a world when there would be no more bondage corruption or decay. It is coming, as surely as day follows night. But we have been called to live in this present world, a world with its corruption that we can and do grow weary of, and long for the world to come.

Paul said in Philippians 1:23 *I am hard pressed between the two: my desire is to depart and be with Christ, for that is far better;* ²⁴*but to remain in the flesh is more necessary for you.* We get the picture of Paul, his body rotting away but his spirit floating around in heaven and that is correct, but it is not all the picture.

Corruption will not win. For there is a resurrection, and there is a glorified body and a new heaven and a new earth. Isaiah was allowed a glimpse of this when he said (Isa: 11:6-9) *"The wolf also shall dwell with the lamb, and the leopard shall lie down with the kid; and the calf and the young lion and the fatling together; and a little child shall lead them. [7]And the cow and the bear shall feed; their young ones shall lie down together: and the lion shall eat straw like the ox. [8]And the sucking child shall play on the hole of the asp, and the weaned child shall put his hand on the cockatrice' den. [9]They shall not hurt nor destroy in all my holy mountain: for the earth shall be full of the knowledge of the LORD, as the waters cover the sea."*

You have been called as a herald of this age to come amidst all this decay. Do not tire in proclaiming Christ's gracious acceptance of sinners, do not tire of warning them of the consequence of spurning the mercy of a loving Saviour.

CONCLUSION

People look at this world with all its trials and sorrows and ask "How can there possibly be a kind and loving God"? It would almost be easier to let our reason govern our faith and believe, that if God did exist that he was rather a diabolical fiend. What is more of a dilemma is that this belief in the goodness of God arose in a time of great cruelty, short lifestyles and none of the advances in medicine and pain relief we now expect.

The pastors to which I delivered these addresses had seen this stark reality of how different life was compared to how it could and should be. Yet despite their doubts and questions they remain faithful. Did these addresses answer all their questions? I doubt it but they left encouraged to trust the God who said he was faithful and whose faithfulness they had tasted on many occasions.

I hope you also found these small addresses to be useful.

www.ingramcontent.com/pod-product-compliance
Lightning Source LLC
Chambersburg PA
CBHW071836020426
42331CB00007B/1742